Skit'omatic

How to Get Up on Stage and Let All Your Creative Personalities Express Themselves as You Use Skits to Teach, Inform and Entertain!

INCLUDES:

- SKITS FOR **EVANGELISM**

- SKITS FOR **ANNOUNCEMENTS**

- SKITS THAT **INVOLVE KIDS IN THE CHURCH**

- **PLUS: ALL THE BASICS** OF SKIT PERFORMING

Compiled by
JUDITH L. ROTH
with contributions by
Duffy Robbins, Lawrence & Andrea Enscoe, Robin Jones Gunn and Many Others!

FROM GOSPEL LIGHT

Editorial Staff
Mark Maddox, Publisher
Gary S. Greig, Ph.D., Senior Editor
Carol Eide, Youth Editor

Design
Ted R. Killian, Senior Designer

Contents

Introducing the Writers

Lawrence G. and Andrea J. Enscoe got married in the midst of writing the skits for this book. Andee has taught theater in both the classroom and seminar setting, and is the co-author of a book of drama for teens. Larry is co-founder of The Harlequin Players and is the author and co-author of numerous books of Christian theater. At U.C. Berkeley he received the Eisner prize for Highest Achievement in Literature.

Robin Jones Gunn is the writer of the "Christy Miller" teen fiction series (Focus on the Family). She has also written twelve books for children and many articles for Christian magazines. Robin is involved in youth ministry with her husband. Part of her ministry is directing the youth drama group.

Barbara D. Larsen is a member of the Ethel Herris Critique Group. She has written several skits and plays for groups to use. Barbara is in the process of writing the script for a music-drama on the life of Peter.

Marco Palmer is the comedic actor and writer for the Gospel Light video, *Sunday Night Live*, as well as for the traveling drama ministry, "The Acts Drama Company." He has toured with "Acts" since 1980, performing in churches, prisons and schools all over the United States and Europe.

Kathy Pocsics has written magazine articles, poetry and several plays and skits. She has been an actress, director and playwright for drama productions at First Evangelical Free Church in Fullerton

Duffy Robbins is chairman of the department of youth ministry for Eastern College. He is a 20-year veteran of youth ministry and has spoken across the country at youth retreats, conventions, conferences and workshops for youth workers. Duffy is an associate staff member of Youth Specialties and has written four books in the area of youth ministry.

Judith L. Roth has been a youth minister and an associate editor at Gospel Light Publications. As a minister, she co-produced and wrote two drama musicals for youth. She has had over a dozen poems published in Christian magazines.

Jim and Lisa Suth have been married seven years and met as original cast members of the Harlequin Players. They have often written and performed sketches at their home church, Fremont Community, in California. They have two daughters, Paige and Erin, who are already budding actresses.

David Swaney is a senior at Biola University. He is majoring in Radio, TV, Film and would like to be involved in the film industry either by writing or directing. He has acted in a student film at Biola.

Using This Book

Copies of the Skits

Purchase of this book includes the right to make copies of the skits for those who will be involved in putting on the skits.

Generic Announcements

Fill in the blanks of these skits with your own announcement information. Choose the skit based on the type of activity you wish to promote. For example, if you wish to announce to the congregation that the youth are doing a car wash to make money to go to camp, turn to the Church Life Announcements section. There you will find a Generic Appeal by Youth skit. This one will fit a car wash announcement.

If you want to announce to the youth group that a Christian concert is coming up, turn to the Youth Group Announcements section. The Generic Youth Activity Announcement can be used to announce the concert.

Skit Features

Each skit contains the following features designed to help you prepare the skit: **Characters, Props** and **Optional** props. The teaching skits also have headings concerning the **Main Theme** with possible Scriptures to use.

Props

Any prop can be replaced by an imaginary one simply by pretending it is there and miming accordingly. If you want to use actual props, the items listed after the "Props" heading are the props that are most necessary. The optional props don't need to be used, but they make the production that much more polished. Another option is to substitute certain props with objects that are more accessible—like using a chair instead of an acting block.

Blackout, Exit

At the end of each skit, you will find a stage direction that looks something like this: *BLACKOUT (freeze, then exit)*. "BLACKOUT" means that if you are using stage lights, they are to be shut off at that point. The directions in the parentheses should be followed if stage lights are not being used. To "freeze, then exit" means to hold the pose for a moment to signal to the audience that the skit is finished. The skit player may then exit the stage, no longer playing their character. For example, if you are playing a child character, don't leave the stage area skipping as a child might. Leave the way you would leave under normal circumstances.

If you are in a room with ordinary lighting, you may want to douse the room lights for a few seconds at the blackout directions to signal the completion of the skit.

Topical Index

To help you find a teaching skit that matches a topic you will be studying, an index has been included that lists major subject headings in alphabetical order.

Skits, Kids and Church Involvement

Getting kids to become followers of Christ is sometimes a lot easier than getting them to become active in a church. They end up stuck on the fringes—in a parachurch ministry or isolated in a youth group. Youth and the rest of the church don't often mix easily.

But kids need the fellowship of the local church. They need to be supported, nurtured and held accountable. They need to find their place in the Body of Christ and in the worshiping community. And churches need the vitality of their young.

That's one of the reasons this book was developed—to provide a resource for increasing youth participation in the activities of their congregation. To give kids a chance to belong.

Following are some reasons why skit participation can make an important difference in the lives of kids and churches:

1. **The more involved kids become, the more they feel they belong.** By being a part of a worship service or other gathering, kids sense their part in the body and respond to it.

2. **Performing skits gives kids a chance to contribute to their church—to use their gifts.** Sometimes kids have a "gimme" attitude because they have never had the opportunity to be the givers. Here is their chance to give.

3. **Taking part in a worship service gets the kids into church.** No small feat sometimes, especially when they don't have church-going parents. And the use of skits in the service will often make the time spent in church more interesting to them.

4. **Being up front brings the kids to the adults' attention in a positive way.** When youth are visible they are less likely to be overlooked and more likely to be considered an important part of the body.

Because of the importance of youth involvement in a worshiping community, there is a section in this book that is especially for all-church gatherings. The ideas and skits in this section will give the kids a chance to be in front of the congregation to do special all-church announcements. The section also contains some possible youth announcement skits that would relate to the whole church.

Most of the skits in the "Skits that Teach" section can be used to help illustrate a sermon or to give a devotional thought. Some skits can be used as children's sermons during worship services.

There is also a section containing skits to be used for evangelization. These skits are written specifically to enable kids to spark an interest in their Savior. To draw the attention of the secular community around each particular church to the reason for the Church—"Christ in you, the hope of glory" (Col. 1:27).

Getting Skittish: Short, Practical Tips

One of the nicest things about skits is that they are easy to prepare. Skits are not often big Broadway-type productions, and that is good news for the harried youth worker trying to minister in these days when even the microwave doesn't seem to work fast enough.

Another nice thing about skits is they can be primped and polished to the hilt when the mood strikes.

A lot or a little—it all depends on how you want to do it. Here are the basics to go on.

Speaking

It's not necessary to have Dustin Hoffman or Meryl Streep in your cast in order to pull off a skit. Good acting is a plus but it's not essential in order to have a fruitful experience. What *is* essential is that the lines are heard by the audience. The performers need to speak slowly and clearly—with their mouths directed at the audience. There are few things more frustrating to an audience than to watch a performance and miss half of the words.

The following exercises improve clarity. While kids may feel silly doing them, if you approach the activities in a lighthearted manner, you'll probably win their cooperation. Tell them to go ahead and laugh. It's good for the diaphragm.

Exercises for loudness:

1. Have the kids stand on stage facing the audience. All together they should yell, shout, belt out a song—in other words, make noise. Tell them to remember how this feels (in their lungs, diaphragm, throat, mouth), and to repeat this action when they are performing so that it feels the same.

2. Using the sound "ha" as their vocalization, have the kids get louder and softer under your direction. Instruct them to keep their faces relaxed—the tension should be in their diaphragms. It may help for them to put their hands to their faces and diaphragms to check out the tension levels there.

Exercises for slowness:

1. Using their arms like a choir director would, the kids should "direct" each syllable of their lines.

2. Time how long it takes each kid to say his or her lines. Then have each one try to double the amount of time they take.

3. Before running through a skit, have kids breathe deeply and relax. They should think, *slow motion.*

Setting the Mood

Mood setting is not a high priority when it comes to skits, but for that little extra (if you have the time and the inclination) try some of these ideas.

Lights: Brighter lights create a stagey look. Dimmer lights create a serious or romantic look. Spotlights give definition, attention. Flashlights, Christmas tree lights or fake campfires are a fun effect.

Music: Background, movie themes, TV themes.

Sound effects: Sound effects can be accomplished by someone making the sounds during the performance, taping sounds beforehand and playing them during the performance, or by using a sound effects album.

Entrances: If it is a serious skit, the performers should not bound onto stage. They should not drag on if the skit is comical. Keep the entrances in tune with the mood.

Costumes/Props

The skit is not a medium for understatement. Because skits are short, the audience needs to recognize the characters and understand the situation immediately. There is no time to waste building a character or situation. If a man enters the stage wearing a cowboy hat and a gun holster and walking bowlegged, the audience knows right away that this is a cowboy, with all the accompanying quirks.

Stereotypes are good tools for quick audience recognition. In full-length endeavors, an old woman with a cane is a cliche. In skits, the cliche prop or costume is one of the quickest and easiest ways to help the audience identify the characters. Keeping a ready supply of tags (props or costumes that identify a character) makes quick skit production easier. A closet or box set side for costumes and prop tags usually will be enough.

Here are some examples of costume/prop tags that may come in handy for use with this skitbook:

Old man/old woman hats, knitting paraphernalia, newspaper, microphone, gaudy jewelry, school backpack, lunch sacks, baby bottle, little kid beanie, glasses, bald "wig," fright wig, telephone, baseball bat, stuffed animals, tool box and flashlights. Actor's blocks are also handy to have around. They are generally square, wooden and about the size of a bass drum; sturdy enough to stand on, light enough to move around and easy to paint.

One inexpensive way to build a wardrobe and prop supply is by asking for donations of "junk" from the church. Another way is by visiting thrift stores and garage sales and buying good deals on everything imaginable from bowling balls to briefcases. Throwing a church yard sale could serve a two-fold purpose—first pick of skit supplies and fund-raising to buy other necessary items.

Makeup

Skits are usually not dramatically formal enough to require makeup. If makeup is necessary (to portray an elderly person or a clown, for example), use these ideas:

1. Put on a cold cream base so that the makeup washes off easily.
2. Sponge foundation on all skin that will be exposed. Use a skin tone, normally. Use whiteface for a clown.
3. Exaggerate facial lines so that they can be seen from a distance.
4. Exaggerate color if bright lights will be used.
5. Use enough powder to set the makeup (so that it does not melt or sweat off easily). Pour some powder the same color as the foundation onto a paper towel. The person with the makeup on should hold the paper towel up to his or her face and, with eyes closed, blow sharply at the powder. It will rise in a cloud and coat the face, setting the makeup.
6. After the performance, take off the makeup by using cold cream and facial tissues

Clowning/Miming

One way to get expert tips on clowning and miming is by inviting a professional troupe to put on a short seminar for your youth. Contact nearby college theater groups or community theater groups to find out if there are any such clowning companies in your area. If you are fortunate enough to have a Christian clowning group near you, take advantage of the opportunity. Some groups perform in churches for a love offering, and may be willing to throw in a seminar at minimal cost.

Other possibilities for instruction are the *Clown Ministry Video* and *Leader's Guide* with Floyd Shaffer, available from Group Books. Four books available from Contemporary Drama Service are: *The Clown Ministry Handbook,* by Janet Litherland; *Send in His Clowns,* by Stephen P. Perrone and James P. Spata; *Mime Ministry,* by Susie Kelly Toomey; and *Clown Act Omnibus,* by Wes McVicar. For these four books, write to: Contemporary Drama Service, Box 7710-TI, Colorado Springs CO, 80933.

Church Life Announcements

Skitting Around with Announcements: Part 1

Unless a stand-up comic makes the announcements in your church, chances are that the time taken to report on church life and coming events is the most uneventful part of your worship service. The following skits and ideas are designed to bring pep into your church's announcement time and to draw attention to those notices that are special.

This section contains skit-like ideas to present your information to the congregation. It also has skits that are written for general church announcements. Customize the general announcements (generic skits) by inserting your specific information into the blanks indicated on the skit scripts. Or present your information using one of the many skit ideas given. There should be at least one skit and several ideas that fit any announcement.

The skits are short so that they are easy to memorize and don't take up much time in the service.

Before the service begins, make sure you've planned the entrance(s) and exit(s) of the skit. Smooth transitions are important. Try to spend as little time as possible getting in position for the announcement so that the flow of the service is not interrupted.

Because of the wacky nature of many skits and sketches, churches that have a formal worship time may not appreciate skits during their regular worship services. If your church fits this description, it might be best to save the wackier skits for more informal settings and youth meetings. Discern what would be appropriate for your congregation. Your minister can help you decide if you are unsure.

These creative methods of sharing information will help improve awareness of and attendance to church activities, involve young people in the worship service and wake up drowsy churchgoers. As you read the following pages, consider how you might use the ideas presented to benefit your youth group and church.

All-Church Announcement Ideas

Visual Impact Announcement

Advance preparation: Staple opposite ends of a white sheet to two long sticks or dowels. Also round up a can of bright paint, a thick paintbrush (about 3 inches wide, or more) and a dropcloth. The "painter" should dress in old clothes.

Skit: Two kids set the dropcloth out on the floor of the announcement area. Two more kids (or the same two) hold the sheet taut by the edges over the drop cloth, holding it up for the congregation to see. The "painter" quickly writes the *basics* of the announcement (event, date, time). For added enjoyment, have appropriate background music playing. (Example: play "Food, Glorious Food" for announcing a barbecue.) If more details are needed, they can be stated during the painting.

Skywriting Announcement

Advance preparation: Write out the basic information about your announcement on a long thin roll of paper. Attach it to the end of a model airplane. Roll the paper into a tube shape.

Skit: One kid enters making airplane noises and maneuvering the model airplane around. He or she unrolls the announcement while moving across the stage. You may need to have someone hold onto the end of the announcement for easier reading. Display it in the back of the church or foyer after the gathering.

Dressed-up Announcement

To draw attention to your announcement, have someone walk down the center aisle (or similar attention-getting place) in "different" attire. The person will either read the announcement or hand it to someone else to read.

Costume possibilities: clown outfit (note will be inside a balloon, pop balloon to read note); tuxedo (note carried on tray); animal costume (note carried in mouth); little girl/boy costume (note pinned to dress/shirt); shipwrecked-on-desert-island outfit (note carried in a bottle); graduate (note is rolled-up diploma); postal worker (note is a letter); town crier (holds out unrolled scroll and calls out announcement).

Mystery Messages

Build interest far in advance of an upcoming event by displaying ambiguous announcements on bulletin boards, in newsletters and in fliers. Verbal announcements may also be used.
Example: "It's coming. LADAPI. Watch for it."

At a chosen time you reveal that "LADAPI" stands for Labor Day Picnic. (Or that "AAUGH!" stands for "Adopt an Unbelievable Grandparent Here!")

Do-It-Thyself Announcement

Write a simple script for the congregation to participate in from their seats. Some ideas are:

Responsive Cheers—For example, "Give me a *W*." "W!" "Give me an *O*." "O!" etc. "What's that spell?" "Workday!" "On what day?" "Saturday!" "At what time?" "Eight o'clock!"

Jingles—Teach them a short song. For example—to the tune of the old Nestle's Quik commercial—"W-O-R-K-D-A-Y, you can make it if you try. Workday."

Team Effort—Split the congregation into two groups. Give each group a different part. For example, one group stands up when it is their turn to say, "Work," the other group stands up when they say, "Day." They would be cued by a leader in a "Simon Says" fashion.

Videotape the congregation as they join in the announcement and play the video for them as they leave the meeting.

Limerick or Poem

Write the announcement as a silly limerick or poem that a youth group member will recite. For example:

The youth group is having a meeting
to decide what to do about seating.
We hope you come, too...
to make sure that you do
we'll provide lots of goodies for eating.

Limericks can be used as introductions to skits, also. An introduction for the following "Old Favorites" idea might be:

There once was a guy from this city
who asked me to sing a small ditty.
My voice is not rad
and the accompaniment is bad
but I'd rather do this than a skitty.

Old Favorites

Choose an old, well-known song and fit your announcement to the tune. Have the whole group sing. For example, this is set to the tune, "I've Been Working on the Railroad":

I've been working on this party
all the live-long day.
I've been working on this party
so we'd have some games to play.
Don't you want to come and be here?
It doesn't start too early in the morn.
Don't you want to come and eat here?
We could have some corn.

We could really eat. (2x)
We could even eat some corn.
(repeat)

Reporter at Large

Arrange to have a cordless microphone or a microphone with a long cord. Have one of your kids play "Reporter-at-Large" by asking congregation members during the announcement time what they know about the subject of this particular announcement. After a few people have been interviewed, the reporter-at-large should fill in any missing elements to the announcement.

Generic All-Church Activity Announcement
Judith L. Roth

Characters
ETHYLL: An old woman
WILBUR: Ethyll's old husband

Props: Two chairs, some knitting, a newspaper. **Optional:** Rocking chairs instead of ordinary chairs.

ETHYLL and WILBUR are in rocking chairs. ETHYLL is knitting. WILBUR has fallen asleep while reading a newspaper.

ETHYLL: Wilbur?

WILBUR (startled awake, drops newspaper on floor): What do you want, old woman?

ETHYLL (peering at him over her glasses): Wilbur, I want you to take me to the (fill in activity) at church on (fill in date, time). Now, none of your excuses. We're going to have a wonderful time.

WILBUR has been trying to reach his newspaper, but for some reason can't get out of his chair.

WILBUR: Well, if I can ever get out of this chair....

ETHYLL: Tch, tch. You always were a lazy old coot but that's the poorest excuse I've ever heard. (Fill in activity) on (fill in date, time). Write it down in your little book.

WILBUR (struggling): No, really, Ethyll. I can't get out of this chair.

ETHYLL (playing along): And I can't get out of mine, either. I guess we'll just have to take them along. It will be just dandy. (Use however much space necessary, if any, to give details about the announcement.)

WILBUR continues struggling comically. ETHYLL peers at him.

Really, Dear. Don't you think you're carrying this a bit too far?

WILBUR (stopping for a breather): I think your grandson must've glued me down.

ETHYLL: Little (fill in name of well-known church rascal)? That sweet boy? Don't be ridiculous. Probably too much apple pie has wedged you in there. Here, let me help.

ETHYLL attempts to rise, but finds she's stuck, too.

ETHYLL: (Name of rascal). You little rascal. When I get my hands on you....

ETHYLL stands up holding chair on backside and begins exiting. WILBUR follows her, doing the same.

(To WILBUR.) Don't think this gets you out of going to (activity).

WILBUR: I know, I know. (Activity) on (date). I'll be there with bells on. They'll be lighter than this old chair, anyway.

BLACKOUT (exit)

13

Generic Social Concern Activity Announcement

Judith L. Roth

Characters
GERONIMO: Talk show host
BEAUFORT: Food fight instigator
VOICE: A person in the audience

Props: A sheet, a dowel, a paper bag, a bright directional light.

A sheet, suspended over a dowel, is hung in front of the audience. BEAUFORT is sitting behind the sheet with his profile toward the audience. VOICE is planted somewhere in the audience. Music comes up as GERONIMO enthusiastically comes onto the platform. Audience claps. Music fades.

GERONIMO (to audience/congregation): We've got a great show for you today. Later on we'll be talking about Japanese beetle water-skiers. Can they really ski in formation? And I'll give you a chance to give your opinion on the packaging of potato chips. Bags or cylinders—it could make a big difference in your life. But now I'd like to bring to your attention the food fight instigator.

Lights come up behind BEAUFORT, projecting a shadow of his profile on the sheet.

Because he wishes to remain anonymous, I'll only be using his first name.

(To BEAUFORT) Beaufort, could you tell us what caused you to throw your entire plate of spaghetti on the ceiling of the (<u>fill in local high school</u>)?

BEAUFORT: I just had a sudden urge to do it. It was terrible, Geronimo. Pretty soon, cole slaw was flying through the air and a small artillery of peas bounced off the back of my head whenever I tried to escape. There were—

VOICE: Hey, why are you hiding behind that sheet?

BEAUFORT: I'm, ah, remaining anonymous because I feel guilty.

VOICE: So you threw a bit of food. What's the big deal?

BEAUFORT: It's not just that....

GERONIMO: What is it, Beaufort?

BEAUFORT (quietly): I, uh, feel guilty because of the wasted food....I guess what I really feel guilty about is that I have so much and so many people have nothing. Oh, I'm so ashamed!

BEAUFORT puts a bag over his head.

GERONIMO (to audience): Did he do what I think he did? (To BEAUFORT) Beaufort, did you just put a bag over your head?

BEAUFORT: I feel so...so worthless!

VOICE: So why don't you do something about it?

BEAUFORT: What could I do?

GERONIMO: For starters, you could get that bag off of your head. We're having a hard time understanding you.

BEAUFORT (taking off bag): What could I do? There's so much wrong, and I'm so busy.

14

VOICE: Well, you could (<u>fill in description and name of activity</u>).

BEAUFORT: When is it?

VOICE: (<u>Fill in date, time</u>).

BEAUFORT: I don't know. I think I have an appointment with my tree surgeon.

GERONIMO: Come on, Beaufort. If you really feel badly about the world situation, the least you could do is (<u>activity</u>).

VOICE: Yeah, wimp. (<u>Fill in activity and time</u>). Be there or be square.

BEAUFORT: Well, I don't know....

GERONIMO: Well, there you have it, folks. The conscience is a terrible thing to waste. And now a word from our sponsor.

(<u>Use this opportunity to give more details about the activity, if necessary.</u>)

BLACKOUT (exit)

Generic Appeal by Youth

Judith L. Roth

Characters
CLARINDA: British Lady of the Manor
JEFFREY: Clarinda's butler

Props: A paperback novel, a box of bonbons, a comfy chair or couch, expensive-looking lounging clothes and jewelry, a butler-like uniform.

CLARINDA is lounging with a paperback novel and a box of bonbons.

JEFFREY enters and waits to be noticed. Finally, he clears his throat. CLARINDA startles.

CLARINDA: What is it, Jeffrey?

JEFFREY: Madame, there are two someones at the door. From (fill in group name).

CLARINDA: Well? What do they want?

JEFFREY: Madame, they want you to (fill in need).

CLARINDA: Don't be ridiculous, Jeffrey. I haven't time for that sort of nonsense. Can't you see I'm busy?

JEFFREY: Of course.

JEFFREY hesitates.

CLARINDA: Is there something else?

JEFFREY: No, Madame. (He hesitates again.) It's—it's just that they seem so sincere. (Fill in details as needed.)

CLARINDA: Jeffrey. Are you presuming to question me?

JEFFREY: No, Madame.

He hesitates. Then draws himself up to his full height.

But if you won't help them then I must prevail upon you to let me go so that I might help them myself.

CLARINDA (shocked): *You*, Jeffrey? You would leave me to (fill in need) for someone you don't even know?

JEFFREY (determined): Yes. I would.

CLARINDA (deflated): Oh.

JEFFREY turns to go. Turns back.

JEFFREY: Although it would be much more smashing if you came along.

CLARINDA (looking away): Do you mean that, Jeffrey?

JEFFREY (eagerly going towards her): Yes, I do, Clarinda. I mean, Madame.

CLARINDA looks at JEFFREY, looks at book, tosses book over her shoulder. She gets up and takes his arm.

CLARINDA (as they exit): Did you really mean *smashing*, Jeffrey?

BLACKOUT (exit)

Generic Church Family Announcement
Judith L. Roth

Characters
ETHYLL: Old woman
WILBUR: Ethyll's old husband

Props: Two chairs, some knitting, one to two dozen cookies, a newspaper, a pencil. **Optional:** Rocking chairs instead of ordinary chairs.

> *ETHYLL and WILBUR are rocking. ETHYLL is knitting. WILBUR is munching cookies under cover of reading the newspaper.*

ETHYLL: Do you hear something strange, Wilbur?

WILBUR: Hm?

ETHYLL: Kind of like the sound of a beaver...gnawing on a wooden nickel.

WILBUR (swallowing quickly): Oh, really. Is that what it sounds like?

> *WILBUR stuffs another cookie in his mouth.*

ETHYLL (getting suspicious): Look at me when I'm talking to you, you old coot.

> *WILBUR takes a pencil from his shirt pocket and pokes two holes through the newspaper. He holds the holes up to his eyes.*

WILBUR: There. I see you, Ethyll.

ETHYLL: What are you up to, old man?

WILBUR (quickly): Well, lookee here (points to article in paper; still hiding behind paper). It says here that (<u>fill in part of announcement</u>).

ETHYLL: Don't change the subject.

WILBUR (going on): (<u>Fill in the rest of announcement.</u>)

> *ETHYLL, meanwhile, gets out of chair and peeks behind his paper. Time this so she shouts as he finishes the announcement.*

ETHYLL: Ah ha!

> *WILBUR jumps. Cookies fly everywhere.*

Thought you could hide from me, did you? Eating those cookies I baked for dear old Mrs. Griswold!

> *As she speaks, ETHYLL stoops and picks up cookies, blowing on them and brushing them off, one by one. WILBUR looks on hungrily.*

WILBUR: Didn't you hear me? (<u>Fill in brief exciting news. Example: Janie had her baby!</u>)

ETHYLL (picking lint off cookies and mumbling): Dumping my good cookies all over the floor.

WILBUR: (<u>Fill in repeat of brief exciting news.</u>) Don't you think this calls for a celebration? How about a celebration of cookies?

ETHYLL (shocked out of her mumbling): I'll "celebration of cookies" you, you old coot.

> *ETHYLL chucks cookies at WILBUR, who exits, shielding himself with the newspaper. ETHYLL follows, still mumbling and pelting him.*
>
> *BLACKOUT (exit)*

Generic Weekly Activity Announcement
Judith L. Roth

Characters
BOB: TV host
DARLA: Bachelorette
BACHELOR #1
BACHELOR #2
BACHELOR #3

Props: Four stools, a divider, three flashlights, a piece of paper. **Optional:** Taped game show music, a cassette recorder.

BACHELORS #1-3 are sitting in a line facing the audience. There is a divider between BACHELORS and the other half of the stage. Catchy music comes up as BOB runs onstage. Music goes down.

BOB: Good day, folks, and welcome to another episode of "The Rating Game." Let's meet our bachelors.

As each BACHELOR is introduced (and later, every time each BACHELOR speaks) each BACHELOR shines a flashlight on his own face for a spotlight effect. Music plays under BOB's descriptions.

Bachelor #1 is 23. He enjoys hiking, biking and striking and is a C.P.A.

Bachelor #2 is 32. He enjoys mooing, booing and chewing. He's a cattle rancher and movie critic.

Bachelor #3 is 75. He enjoys walking, talking and rocking and is a retired soap opera star.

Now that you've met our bachelors, let's bring out our Bachelorette. Come on out, Darla.

DARLA enters carrying a page of questions and waves at the audience.

DARLA: Hi Bob.

BOB: Hi Darla. Let me explain the rules to you one more time. You may ask each bachelor one question, then you must rate each bachelor. The one with the highest rating will go on a date with you, compliments of "The Rating Game." Any questions?

DARLA: No.

BOB: Okay, you may begin.

DARLA (referring to her notes): Bachelor #1—What is an activity you do every week?

BACHELOR #1: Well, Darla, every week I go to (fill in activity). It's on (fill in day of the week) at (fill in time). It's the best.

DARLA: Thank you, Bachelor #1. Bachelor #2—same question.

BACHELOR #2: Darla, I have to agree with Bachelor #1. I go to (fill in activity) every week without fail. It (fill in description of benefits of activity).

DARLA: Oh. Thanks, Bachelor #2. Bachelor #3? Do you have anything different you do every week?

BACHELOR #3: Well, golly, I wish I did, but those other two bachelors stole my answer. I go to (fill in activity) every week, too. I guess you'll just have to choose between us by who has the purtiest voice.

BOB: There are your answers, Darla. How do they rate?

DARLA: They were all the same, Bob. How am I supposed to choose?

BOB: Eenie meenie minie moe?

DARLA: Not funny, Bob.

BOB (to audience): While Darla is deciding, let me tell you about the exciting date we have planned for her and her lucky bachelor. An all-expenses paid trip to (<u>fill in weekly activity</u>). She and her lucky bachelor will (<u>fill in description of what goes on at the activity</u>). Afterward, we will treat the whole gang to an ice cream cone at 4,891 flavors. (To DARLA.) Won't that be great?

DARLA: Well, if we're going to (<u>fill in activity</u>), it doesn't matter who I choose. They're all going to be there.

BOB: I won't be there.

DARLA: You might as well be. So I'll take *you.*

> DARLA puts her arm through BOB's and escorts him offstage.

BOB (to BACHELORS): Sorry, guys. See you at (<u>fill in activity</u>). (To audience) And see you tomorrow on "The Rating Game."

> Music comes up as BACHELORS exit carrying their chairs and mumbling things like "Hmph" and "Well, of all the nerve."
>
> BLACKOUT (exit)

Skitting Around with Announcements: Part 2

There's something about a lively performance that grabs attention—even the attention of a roomful of teenagers. If your announcement times are spent fending off paper airplanes and struggling to make your message heard above the gossip corner chatter, try couching your announcement in a skit. Then let the kids who were involved with the skit answer the numerous, "What time did you say it starts?" and, "How much does it cost again?" questions. Chances are the announcement will really be heard and your throat may be saved in the process.

This section contains skit-like ideas to present your information to the youth group in a creative way. It also contains skits that are written for general youth announcements. Customize the general announcements (generic skits) by inserting your specific information into the blanks indicated on the skit scripts. Or present your information using one of the many skit ideas given. There should be at least one skit and several ideas that fit any announcement.

The skits are short to be easy to prepare and so that not too much time is taken from the rest of your program.

It may be best to have the skits kick off the program so that the kids involved can be ready and waiting—that way they won't miss anything or give away any surprises.

Engineer the beginning of each skit so that it looks like a classy production. Kids can be very critical, so it is important to impress them from the start. They appreciate a job well done. All of your skit players should know exactly when to come in and where to stand. Make sure they practice where they will perform so that any space problems can be worked out. Another important thing for them to remember to do is to have fun. If they can relax and enjoy what they are doing, their audience will relax and enjoy, too.

Youth Meeting Announcement Ideas

Dummy Announcement

In advance, choose a small teen from the group. With a dark makeup pencil, draw lines from the corner of the kid's mouth down to the jawbone. Have him or her sit on your knee and act like a ventriloquist's dummy. While you try to say the announcements without moving your lips, the "dummy" tries to move his or her mouth at the same time.

Arms to Spare

Give announcements doing the old trick of using someone else's arms as your own. There are several ways of doing this.

1. Both people wear the same color shirts. One person stands facing the group, holding her arms behind her. The other person stands in back of the first and puts her arms under the front person's arms and out in front. The person in back acts as the arms of the person in front by making appropriate gestures as the front person gives the announcements.
2. Get a sweatshirt or other shirt big enough to go over two people. The front person holds her arms out of the way. The back person's arms go through the sleeves.
3. Follow the instructions for number two, but place a table in front of the pair. The front person wears shoes on her hands and makes appropriate foot gestures on the table with them.

Charade Ready-made

Divide the group into two teams. Write down on separate pieces of paper the titles of songs, movies, TV shows or books that have a word of your announcement on them. For example:

Ernest Goes to Camp	(Activity)
One Hundred and One Dalmations	(Cost)
"thirtysomething"	(Date)
"Tomorrow"	(Sign-up Deadline)

Hand the first piece of paper to a player from Team 1. That person acts out the message to his or her own team. When the team guesses it, write the word for your announcement on the board. Hand the second message to a player from Team 2, and so on. Time how long it takes each team to guess correctly. When the charades are finished, fill in any necessary details. These charades will help the kids remember the main points of the announcements better. You may want to let the team with the least time get a discount on the activity just announced.

Big Splash

This announcement should be performed outdoors.

Preparation: On a white sheet paint in large letters with white oil-based paint the name of the subject of your announcement (examples: car wash, concert, retreat). Let it dry completely. Enlist two people to dress up like clowns to help you with the announcement.

Have two volunteers hold the sheet on either side, keeping it taut. Let these two in on the skit so that they know not to drop the sheet. Make sure the announcement is right side up and that it is facing the group so that the sun is not shining from behind it. Other than the two who are holding it, the kids should not be close enough to the sheet to be able to see the white paint. Pretend that the sheet is a backdrop for the clown act.

The clowns come from behind the sheet, each carrying two buckets. Both clowns have in one of their buckets water dyed brightly with bright-colored food coloring. In the other bucket, one clown has plain water; the other has confetti. They put on a typical, "Don't bug me or I'll douse you" clown skit. Finally, the clown with plain water douses the other clown. The doused clown takes his or her pail of dyed water to douse the other clown and gets the sheet instead. The remaining pail of dyed water is also thrown at the sheet, so that the entire word painted there shows up white against a colored background.

The clowns decide to get the audience, and one grabs the pail of confetti (which kids should assume is water) and "douses" the audience with confetti.

This is a splashy way to introduce an announcement.

Doggie News

Enlist someone's big friendly dog. Write an announcement boldly on both sides of a sandwich board type of apparatus. (You may want to use folded cardboard or part of an old sheet.) Attach the apparatus across the back of the dog so that the announcement is displayed on either side of the dog. Or write the announcement on helium balloons that are attached to the dog's collar. Have the dog roam among the kids before the meeting begins.

Network News

(This requires a video camera that uses the same size video tape as the VCR.)

Using a VCR, tape the opening music and logo of a news program. Just as the anchor person is about to come on the screen, stop the tape, put it in your video camera and tape yourself (seated at a "news desk") saying, "Good evening. Our major story tonight is...."

Insert your announcements.

Job Kabob

Go to various places where kids from your youth group work. With a video camera, film the kids announcing upcoming youth activities. For example, ask a kid who works at a fast food restaurant to talk about how good the food will be at camp. Ask someone who works at a clothing store to speak about proper attire for the event.

Masked Announcer

Choose one of your more responsible youth group members to be "The Masked Announcer." Have him or her dress as Zorro and wield a felt marker "sword." The victim, a male who has been clued in ahead of time, is dressed in expendable light-colored clothing. The victim should be doing announcements or something that requires him to be in front of the group. The Masked Announcer enters with a seeming surprise attack. Quickly, in typical swordplay, The Masked Announcer writes information pertinent to an important announcement all over the clothes of the victim. Legibility is not necessary. The Masked Announcer makes a dramatic getaway when finished. The victim play-acts surprise during the attack, and afterwards interprets the hieroglyphics all over his clothing. During the rest of the meeting, he will be a living announcement of the special event.

Generic Youth Activity Announcement
Judith L. Roth

Characters
DEZI: Teenage girl
SHERI: Dezi's friend
NELSON: A wanna-be surfer

Props: School books. **Optional:** One or two backpacks.

> *DEZI and SHERI are in the middle of a discussion on their school campus. They are heading home and have school books either in backpacks or in their arms.*

DEZI: So I told him no, like I'm not part of his car or something, and if he wanted to see me, he'd better crawl out from under his hood and *see* me.

SHERI: And what did *he* say?

DEZI: He said, "There's never anything to do, anyway, so what's the big deal?"

SHERI: What does he mean by that?

DEZI: I don't know. He was just acting like a jerk. So I told him, "Look, if it's that hard for you to plan a simple date, I'll do it for you." And I told him about (fill in the youth group activity).

> *NELSON is walking by as DEZI tells about the activity.*

NELSON: Hey, Dez, did you hear about that, too? Man, surf city!

DEZI: What are you talking about?

NELSON: The youth group is going to (fill in the activity). We're gonna catch some waves, Dude. I mean, Dudette.

SHERI: Nelson, did someone borrow your brain to make pea soup? We're going to (fill in details), not surf.

NELSON: Well, like that's way radical, Dude. And maybe if I bring my board along I can catch some waves.

DEZI (giving up): Yeah. Maybe.

NELSON: And like, since it's during school, you know, I'll come anyway, even if the surf's bad.

SHERI: It's not during school, you nimrod. It's (fill in time and/or date). At (fill in place). Which is miles from the beach, if that makes any difference.

NELSON: Hey, I'm cool. I don't need a beach to surf. Just waves.

Generic Maturing-in-Your-Faith Activity Announcement
Judith L. Roth

Characters
HUEY: An immature Christian teenager
JOSH: Huey's friend
SARA, LEE, LORNA and DOON: Huey's wish list of girlfriends

Props: Lunch sacks, lunch food, a teen-sized diaper, a baby bottle, a tape of "Fat Baby," a tape player.
Optional: Baby bonnet, rattle, rubber duckie.

> *SARA, LEE, LORNA and DOON are brown-bagging it in their school lunch area. HUEY enters wearing nothing but a large diaper over a pair of shorts. He has a bottle in one hand. Other costume accessories for HUEY might be: a baby bonnet, a rattle, a rubber duckie. LORNA sees HUEY.*

LORNA (calling to HUEY): Hi, cutie-pie. Where've you been? Want to eat lunch with us?

HUEY (trying to be cool): I don't know. Some of the cheerleaders wanted me to eat with them. (He pauses.) What the heck. I might as well give you girls the pleasure of my company.

SARA (faking sweetness): How condescending of you.

HUEY (modestly): I try my best. Hey, what are you guys doing Saturday night? I'm gonna have a party at my house. No parents, but plenty of other stuff. (He waves his bottle.) Want to come?

> *The girls look uncomfortable.*

LEE: Sorry. I'm baby-sitting.

LORNA: I've gotta study.

DOON: I'm going out with Josh. Somewhere else.

HUEY: You mean Josh won't come, either? (He turns to SARA.) How about you, Sexy?

SARA (choking): I have to wash my cat.

HUEY (takes a long pull on his bottle; to SARA): You don't like me, do you?

LEE: Huey, don't—

SARA: I like you fine. It's just...the way you act sometimes.

DOON (trying to break the tension): Hey, there's Josh.

HUEY (eager to get away): Oh, I need to talk to him. See you guys later.

> *JOSH enters as HUEY runs over to him.*

HUEY: Josh, you've gotta help me. I'm dying over there.

JOSH: What's the matter, Bud?

HUEY: Okay, here's the thing. I know some of those girls like me—they tickle me under the chin and play "This Little Piggy" with me and all. But whenever I ask them to go anywhere, none of them wants to go. You're in with Doon. Do they ever talk about me? What's the deal?

JOSH: Well, I did hear them talking once. About you. I'm not sure you want to hear it.

HUEY (getting down on his knees and clasping his hands together): Oh, I do I do I do. *Tell* me.

JOSH: Okay. They were like, um, rating the guys in the school.

HUEY: They do that, too?

JOSH: Not exactly the same, but kinda. And Lee brought up you...and they agreed you were kind of cute, but....

HUEY: What! But what!

JOSH: Well, it was like this....

> *Music to "Fat Baby," from Amy Grant's* Age to Age *begins playing. The girls get up from their lunch and lip-synch the song. SARA takes the lead, the others sing back-up. Choreograph it with motions like the Lennon Sisters may have used or with soft shoe dancing. When the girls finish singing, they sit down and resume eating.*

HUEY: Oh, this is worse than I thought. They think I'm like a baby?

JOSH: Well, you know you've been a Christian for as long as the rest of us, but for some reason, you're still wearing diapers.

HUEY: I am? (He looks down at his diaper.) Oh my gosh! I am! What am I gonna do?

JOSH: Well, for starters, you could start coming to (fill in the name of the spiritual activity you are trying to promote).

HUEY: Hm. When is it?

JOSH: (Fill in the time and the day[s].)

HUEY (whining): But that's when I watch MTV.

JOSH (sarcastically): That *is* a dilemma.

HUEY: Yeah.

> *HUEY looks over at the girls and suddenly remembers he's wearing a diaper. He begins to pull at it.*

Oh my gosh. This diaper! Do you think the girls noticed?

JOSH: What are you doing? You can't just take it off. (He propels HUEY towards the exit.) Go get some decent clothes, first.

HUEY: Yeah, I guess you're right. When's that thing, again?

JOSH: (Fill in the name)? It's at (fill in times and days). We meet at (fill in place).

HUEY: And the girls?

JOSH: Yeah, they'll be there. But you're gonna get more out of it than just seeing them.

HUEY: Like what?

> *JOSH takes HUEY's bottle and tosses it up in the air as they walk toward the exit.*

JOSH: Ever had steak?

> *HUEY shakes his head.*
>
> *BLACKOUT (exit)*

Generic Camp Announcement
Judith L. Roth

You may use all of the sketches intermittently during one youth meeting, or one once a week, or use however many you choose in whatever way you choose. Make up your own to add to these, if you like.

Characters
SUPERSTUPENDOUS GIRL
BATBOY
DAUGHTER OF TARZAN
TARZAN
FRANKENSTEIN JR.
ANNOUNCER

Props: A T-shirt with a big *S* on it, a huge pad of paper, a pencil, a Batman T-shirt, a bat, jungle attire, a banana, a dark suit, machine bolts. **Optional:** A huge pencil, foliage.

First Announcement
SUPERSTUPENDOUS GIRL, wearing a shirt with a big S on it, faces the audience.

SUPERSTUPENDOUS GIRL: Know what? I'm getting tired of the same routine all the time. Wearing this silly suit, fighting crime, leaping moderate buildings with a single spring. And keeping my identity a secret. What a strain. I need a break!

ANNOUNCER (offstage, sounding like a person who announces the prizes people have won on game shows): Try this! An all expenses payable trip to lovely (<u>fill in the name of the camp or retreat place</u>) nestled in the lovely (<u>name of mountains, hills or valleys</u>) near the lovely (<u>name of ocean, lake, puddle</u>) under the lovely (<u>name of nearby town or city</u>) skies. You will have (<u>fill in number of days</u>) wonderful days and (<u>fill in number of nights</u>) wonderful nights to get away from it all! What could be better? All gourmet meals are included in the price. You won't want to miss a single one! And to help you enjoy your special trip, (<u>fill in approximate number of kids who will attend</u>) kids will join you, making this the best break of your life. Sign up now! What are you waiting for?

SUPERSTUPENDOUS GIRL: What *am* I waiting for? Where do I sign?

She is tossed a huge pad of paper and an enormous pencil from offstage. While she signs up, the ANNOUNCER speaks.

ANNOUNCER: Hey, all of you out there in TV land, you can come, too. Just send (<u>fill in amount of registration or complete cost</u>) to (<u>fill in name of registrar</u>) at (<u>fill in name of church/organization and address</u>). That's (<u>repeat zip code</u>). Or call me at (<u>fill in phone numbers</u>). Once again, that's (<u>repeat phone numbers</u>).

SUPERSTUPENDOUS GIRL (to audience): What are you waiting for?

Second Announcement
BATBOY is wearing a Batman™ T-shirt and carrying at least one bat. He faces the audience.

BATBOY: Ever get tired of the same old routine? Boy, I sure do. Like I think of my dad, Batmister. He's out there wearing weird clothes and driving a neat-o car and smashing up bad guys. What do I get to do?

Good ol' Batboy has to stay in the dugout and pass out bats to a bunch of gross baseball players. What a job. I could really use a break.

ANNOUNCER (offstage, sounding like a person who announces the prizes people have won on game shows): Well, why don't you try this! An all expenses payable trip to neat-o (fill in the name of the camp or retreat place) nestled in the neat-o (name of mountains, hills or valleys) near the neat-o (name of ocean, lake, puddle) under the neat-o (name of nearby town or city) skies. You will have (fill in number of days) wowie-zowie days and (fill in number of nights) wowie-zowie nights to get away from it all! What could be better? All meals are included in the price. And probably a bunch of soda pop, too! And to help you enjoy your fun-filled trip, (fill in approximate number of kids who will attend) kids will join you, making this the bestest break of your life. Sign up now! What are you waiting for?

BATBOY: Hey, yeah! What *am* I waiting for? Where do I sign?

BATBOY is tossed a huge pad of paper and enormous pencil from offstage. While he signs, the ANNOUNCER speaks.

ANNOUNCER: Hey, all of you out there in TV land, you can come, too. Just send (fill in amount of registration or complete cost) to (fill in name of registrar) at (fill in name of church/organization and address). That's (repeat zip code). Or call me at (fill in phone numbers). Once again, that's (repeat phone numbers).

BATBOY: You might as well come. I'm going to be there.

Third Announcement

DAUGHTER OF TARZAN is wearing leopard skin or other jungle attire and eating a banana. She has some sort of foliage in her hair as decoration. TARZAN gives his call from offstage.

DAUGHTER OF TARZAN: It's a drag hanging around in the jungle all day. (She motions with the banana.) Eating chimp food. You know what it's like to get a Big Mac Attack when you're thousands of miles away from civilization? Awful, that's what it is. Dad won't stop yodeling and I keep getting vine juice underneath my fingernails. Really gross. I need to get away.

ANNOUNCER (offstage, sounding like a person who announces the prizes people have won on game shows): Hey, try this! An all expenses payable trip to fabulous (fill in the name of the camp or retreat place) nestled in the fabulous (name of mountains, hills or valleys) near the fabulous (name of ocean, lake, puddle) under the fabulous (name of nearby town or city) skies. You will have (fill in number of days) super-cool days and (fill in number of nights) super-cool nights to get away from it all! What could be better? All non-chimp meals are included in the price. And if you're lucky, you'll even get some junk food. And to help you enjoy your get-away trip, (fill in approximate number of kids who will attend) kids will join you, making this the gnarliest break of your entire life. Sign up now! What are you waiting for?

DAUGHTER OF TARZAN: I don't know. What am I waiting for?

TARZAN (doing a Tarzan-type call from offstage): Aaaaaaaaaaah!

DAUGHTER OF TARZAN: Okay, I'm convinced. Where do I sign?

DAUGHTER OF TARZAN is tossed a huge pad of paper and enormous pencil from offstage. While she signs, the ANNOUNCER speaks.

ANNOUNCER: Hey, all of you out there in TV land, you know, you can come, too. Just send (fill in amount of registration or complete cost) to (fill in name of registrar) at (fill in name of church/organization and address). That's (repeat zip code). Or call me at (fill in phone numbers). Once again, that's (repeat phone numbers).

DAUGHTER OF TARZAN: Face it. We need a break.

Fourth Announcement

FRANKENSTEIN JR. wears a dark suit and has machine bolts coming out of the sides of his forehead. He faces the audience.

FRANKENSTEIN JR.: Sometimes it's just too much. All the stupid comments I hear—(mimicking) "Hey, squarehead, are your bolts on too tight?" And they walk around like my dad used to (he puts his arms straight out in front of him and walks with lurching steps) before he took ballet lessons. Hey, that's history. You know, life is okay, but sometimes I just need a break from the morons around here. A long break.

ANNOUNCER (offstage, sounding like a person who announces the prizes people have won on game shows): How about this?! An all expenses payable trip to the excellent (fill in the name of the camp or retreat place) nestled in the excellent (name of mountains, hills or valleys) near the excellent (name of ocean, lake, puddle) under the excellent (name of nearby town or city) skies. You will have (fill in number of days) perfect days and (fill in number of nights) perfect nights to get away from it all! What could be better? All meals are included in the price. But don't bolt them down, har har. And to help you enjoy your home-away-from-home, (fill in approximate number of kids who will attend) kids will join you, making this the most ironic break of your entire life. Sign up now! What are you waiting for?

FRANKENSTEIN JR.: I guess I'm waiting for an enormous pad of paper to be thrown at me.

ANNOUNCER: Well, here it is!

FRANKENSTEIN JR. is tossed the huge pad of paper and enormous pencil from offstage. While he signs, the ANNOUNCER speaks.

ANNOUNCER: Hey, all of you out there in TV land, you know, you can come, too. Just send (fill in amount of registration or complete cost) to (fill in name of registrar) at (fill in name of church/organization and address). That's (repeat zip code). Or call me at (fill in phone numbers). Once again, that's (repeat phone numbers).

FRANKENSTEIN JR.: Hey, get away. You'll be glad you did.

Generic Missions Opportunity Announcement
Judith L. Roth

Characters
JACKIE: Teenage Christian
STEPHANIE: Teenage Christian

Props: A bed with frilly covering, pillows, dolls, stuffed animals.

>*JACKIE and STEPHANIE are sitting on STEPHANIE's frilly bed which is covered with pillows, dolls and stuffed animals. STEPHANIE has a pillow over her face.*

JACKIE: I sense you are uncomfortable with this idea.

STEPHANIE (uncovering her head long enough to moan): Aaaugh. No, let me put it this way—*Aaaugh!* (She puts the pillowcase over her head.)

JACKIE: So what don't you like about it?

>*STEPHANIE makes little motions with her fingers like bugs flying around. She slaps at herself.*

You're going crazy. No, that's not what you mean. You're afraid you'll fall asleep. No?

>*STEPHANIE takes off the pillow. She adds buzzing to her motions.*

I get it! You're afraid of flying kazoos!

STEPHANIE: You are so dense! Bugs! I'm afraid of bugs!

JACKIE: You think bugs automatically go with the word "missions"?

>*STEPHANIE nods her head emphatically.*

Oh. Well, think about it this way. A mission trip to Hawaii doesn't sound like a hardship, does it? But there are humongous bugs there.

STEPHANIE: Well, count me out of Hawaii, then.

JACKIE: Steph, there are bugs *here*. Probably in your very bed. Probably on your very own Snookie doll.

STEPHANIE (shocked): No! (She picks up her Snookie doll gingerly and examines it.) No bugs on Snookie.

JACKIE: Let me explain it to you again. (Fill in what the mission opportunity is all about.)

STEPHANIE: When is it?

JACKIE: (Fill in dates, times.)

STEPHANIE: I knew it. Prime bug season.

JACKIE: Give me a break. Look, I'll personally be your bug guard. If you see a bug, I'll kill it for you.

STEPHANIE: Gross!

JACKIE: I'll do it neatly where you can't see it.

STEPHANIE: Hm. How much does it cost?

JACKIE: The bug?

STEPHANIE: No! The (fill in mission opportunity).

JACKIE: (Fill in cost, if any.)

STEPHANIE: Is bug spray included in that price?

JACKIE: I'll buy you some, all right?

STEPHANIE: You're leaving something out. I can tell. There's something icky about this that you're not telling me.

JACKIE: (Fill in the rest of the details.) Nothing icky.

STEPHANIE: I think you want me to go because you're afraid of facing those bugs by yourself.

JACKIE (sarcastically): You found me out. Okay. You're right. The reason I want you to go is so that when a teeny tiny spider is a hundred feet away, you will come to my rescue and stomp on it. Right. (Tone changes to normal.) The reason I want you to go is because it's going to be great.

STEPHANIE: Well, okay, I guess. If you promise to be my bug guard.

JACKIE: Cross my heart and hope to find a tarantula.

STEPHANIE: Jackie!

JACKIE: Okay, okay, just kidding! You'll see. It's going to be the best. Um, one more thing.

STEPHANIE: Yeah?

JACKIE (teasing): Could we take your Snookie doll along for a security blanket?

> *STEPHANIE bops JACKIE over the head with her pillow.*
>
> *BLACKOUT (freeze, then exit)*

Generic Preview of the Youth Group's Coming Attractions
Judith L. Roth

(If you would like the sheet music for the songs used in this skit, check your local music store for collections of 50s and early 60s music.)

Characters
MYRON: A brainy teen nerd with a nasal voice
BUZZ: A letterman
BOBBYSOXERS: Three girl back-up singers

Props: Fifties clothes for all the characters, a huge book, a pen.

> *Set in the 1950s. MYRON is carrying a huge book, trying to find a comfortable way to hold it while leafing through it. BUZZ walks by, does a double-take and stops to talk to MYRON.*

BUZZ: Hey, Myron, what *is* that? A record of all your girlfriends?

MYRON (embarrassed): Oh no, Buzz. I don't like girls yet. This is my 50-year planning calendar.

BUZZ: You're already planning for the next 50 years?

MYRON: Oh yes. Here, let me show you. (He flips through several pages.) See, in three years I have my first date.

BUZZ (kidding): You think you'll like girls by then?

MYRON (checking the book): Well, it says I like them just a little, but not enough to kiss them. (He checks again.) I hold my first date's hand. (Checks again.) Gingerly.

BUZZ: It's good to know our leaders of the future are so well-organized.

MYRON: Oh yes, Buzz. It is. So how are *your* plans coming?

BUZZ (looking at his watch): I plan to meet Clarisse in about ten minutes. That's as far as my plans go.

MYRON: Oh. So you like girls already.

BUZZ (pausing in amazement): Yeah. Yeah, I do.

> *MYRON nods and makes a note in his book.*

Clarisse is going to pick me up in her T-bird. We're gonna have fun, fun fun!

MYRON: 'Til her daddy takes her T-bird away.

BUZZ (looking at MYRON strangely): I suppose that's a possibility.

MYRON (tapping his book): Trust me. It is.

BUZZ (looking at his watch again): Well, as long as I'm waiting, why don't you tell me what the youth group has planned for this year.

MYRON (flipping wildly through his book): Oh, that's a good question. I've got a *lot* of information on that. Just let me find the page....Here it is. The youth group's activities for the coming year. My, my, my.

BUZZ: So tell me already.

> *(The next section must be filled in by you, depending on what your plans are for the year.*

Following is a list of possibilities and the corresponding songs that MYRON will sing the catch phrase to. [Whenever MYRON sings, three BOBBYSOXERS pop out from backstage and sing with him, doing choreography together.] Intersperse activities that have no corresponding songs with ones that do.)

Barbecue—Sing the phrase, "Smoke gets in your eyes" from "Smoke Gets in Your Eyes" by Kern and Harbach.

Beach Party—Change the words, "Barbara Anne" to "Come get a tan" in the opening to "Barbara Anne" by Fred Fassert.

Bible Study—Sing the chorus of "Book of Love" by Davis, Patrick and Malone.

Boating Event—Change the word, "Go" to "Row" in the chorus of "Johnny B. Goode" by Chuck Berry.

Bowling—Change the word, "Strolling" to "Bowling" in the chorus of "The Stroll" by Otis and Lee.

Camp—Change the words, "Get a job" to "Summer (winter) camp" in the chorus of "Get a Job" (perhaps better known as "Sha Na Na") by The Silhouettes.

Concert—Change the words, "Barbara Anne" to "Come hear the band" in the opening to "Barbara Anne" by Fred Fassert.

Grad Party—Sing the chorus of "That'll Be the Day" by J. Allison, N. Petty and B. Holly.

Missions Opportunity (overseas or foreign)—Sing "A Thousand Miles Away" by Sheppard and Miller.

Racing Event—Sing the chorus of "Johnny B. Goode," by Chuck Berry.

Retreat—Change the word, "Runaway" to "Hideaway" in the chorus of "Runaway," by Del Shannon and Crook.

Walkathon—Change the word, "Rock" to "Walk" in the chorus of "Rock Around the Clock" by Jimmy DeKnight and Max C. Freedman.

Worship—Sing "Crying in the Chapel" by Artie Glenn.

(Following is an example of how to put this part of the sketch together:)

MYRON: The year will be kicked off with (he sings the chorus to "Get a Job" using the words, "Winter Camp").

BUZZ: Winter camp, huh? Then what?

MYRON (checking his book): Oh! The youth group is going to put on the Easter sunrise service.

BUZZ: Cool. What else?

MYRON: (Sings "Bowling" to the tune of "Strolling.")

(Have MYRON play the songs to the hilt. BUZZ should be responding to MYRON patiently, as one would to a harmless lunatic. During the last event that MYRON announces, there should be something mentioned that wasn't around in the 1950s. If you will be showing a video, that would be a good event for MYRON to announce last. Other ideas to announce last are: new amusement parks, strange-sounding band names or something having to do with new technology, current events or fads. If everything you have planned for the next year was around during the 1950s, have MYRON mention a new soft drink or food that might be at a planned activity—like chicken fajitas.)

BUZZ: Wait a minute. What did you say?

MYRON: (Repeats last thing he said.)

BUZZ: What's that?

MYRON (looking it up): It says here it's (fill in definition).

> *They both look puzzled.*

BUZZ: Let me see that. (He takes the book.)

> Myron, this is the planned activities for the year 199_. Not 1957.

> > *MYRON sings the catch phrase from "Ain't That a Shame," by Fats Domino and Bartholomew. The BOBBYSOXERS pop out to do back-up.*

> By the way, who are those girls?

> > *As MYRON turns to look, the girls exit.*

MYRON: What girls?

BUZZ: Never mind. So what are you doing with plans for the youth group in 199_? Won't you ever graduate?

MYRON (referring to book): I'll either be a youth minister, or held back because of a low socialization aptitude. My book isn't clear.

BUZZ: Well, are you going to like girls by then?

> > *MYRON reads, gets a terrified look on his face and slams the book shut.*

MYRON (quietly): Oh yes.

BUZZ: Can I see what it says?

MYRON: No. It's far too embarrassing.

BUZZ: Oh, come on. (He grabs for the book, MYRON resists and runs off with BUZZ chasing him.) What does it *say*?

> > *BLACKOUT (exit)*

Why Skits Make an Impact

Every good teacher knows that there are different ways of teaching the same thing. Some techniques are more effective than others. And if you want what you're teaching to make an impact, you use an effective technique.

What puts the medium of the skit in this category? Following are some reasons why skits are effective teaching tools[*]:

1. **A skit gets people's attention.** Drama, skits, creativity—these are all attention-getting devices. It makes sense that it's easier to teach if you have the students' attention.

2. **Laughter makes people receptive.** Besides humor being attention-getting, this common element in skits helps us let down our guard and respond to the humorist and what it is he or she is saying. It also makes the lesson seem less preachy.

3. **Skits are a pleasant distraction.** If we are distracted, we don't put up our guard against the information being shared and we don't try to make up reasons why the lesson may be unacceptable to us.

4. **Role-tending and role-playing help people internalize what is taught.** A person who role-tends—which is what a person watching a skit is doing—is much more likely to believe what is being taught is true than the person who is simply lectured to. A person who role-plays—what your students will be doing when they practice and perform a skit—is even more likely than the role-tender to believe that what is being taught is true.

5. **A story can be a neatly packaged lesson.** It's easy to take away with you. People usually remember an illustration—which a skit is—better than they remember an abstract statement. And since your goal is to teach, you probably are interested in the lesson being remembered for some time to come.

Understanding why skits can coax a teachable spirit may help you to use them more effectively in your ministry. For instance, if you know that the performers are affected even more than the audience, you may want to assign certain roles to kids who could benefit from learning that particular lesson.

So put away your lecture notes and let the skits begin!

[*] The following ideas on communicating are adapted from Em Griffin's, *The Mind Changers: The Art of Christian Persuasion* (Tyndale House Publishers, 1984). You may want to read the book for more ideas on communicating your faith in a manner that is well received and effective.

Love Letters

Lawrence G. and Andrea J. Enscoe

Main Theme: Jesus loves us and died for us.
You may want to use this skit as part of a study of John 15:12,13; Ephesians 3:16-19 or 5:2.

Character
PAIGE WESLEY: An older teen

Props: Frumpish girl's clothing, glasses, rumpled clothes, books, magazines, small box, padlock, necklace, key, enough letters to fill the box, letters tied together with ribbon.

PAIGE WESLEY, dressed in a frumpish way with glasses and messy hair, sits center. She's nervous and embarrassed.

PAIGE: I...ah...I have this quirk. This...this thing that I do. (Laughs.) Well, it's way strange. (Pause.) Oh, yeah. Hi, I'm Paige Wesley. Anyways. I guess I'll tell you about it. Wait here.

She goes offstage. After a moment, rumpled clothes and books start to fly onto the stage from where she exited. PAIGE comes back out.

Sorry. My room's a pigsty. Hold on a sec.

She goes back out. More clothes, books and magazines are thrown out onto the stage. She comes back in carrying a small box with a huge padlock on it.

This is it.

She sits down, looks in her pocket. Remembers the key is on her necklace. Opens the box.

Like I said, here it is. What I do.

She pulls out a handful of letters that are creased, folded, taped and torn—letters with hearts and lipstick kisses.

I...well, I collect love letters. Bizarre, huh? I started in the seventh grade and I can't stop. When letters pass, you know, hand to hand across the class? They stop with me. Weepy freshmen tear them up and toss them in the wastebasket? I fish 'em out and tape 'em up.

PAIGE holds up a bunch of letters tied together with ribbon.

Look at these. My favorite in the collection. The love letters to Joanie Buckwood. The whole 10th-grade worth. I paid $20 for the set. Six different guys! She was phenomenal!

She puts them back.

You learn a lot about human nature in these letters. Oh, the power and fragileness of love. The passion and deeds of attraction! The poetry of the human heart. Here's one. (Holds up letter to read.)

Yo, Pookie—Thanks for doing my algebra all last semester. You're a way cool babe. Stay that way. Love, Rodney. P.S. I love your figures.

Oh! I bet they get married. Rodney and Pookie! All that math homework together! (Looks through the box.) Oh, here's a good one. Two lipstick lips, 15 X's, 12 O's, one SWAK and hearts all around the border. Must've taken her all of English class to do this. (Reads letter.)

Dear Mark, To love you as I do now, I must have loved you forever. Everything I see, even though I've seen it a million times, is fresh and new because I have you in my life. I will only ever love you, my Snookums. I hope I can see you after Mr. Puchalski's class today. Love, Kelley.

Sighs and puts it back. Finds another.

Oh, yeah. this one's killer. (Reads letter.)

Michelle, I would do anything for you. I would buy you anything. Go anywhere. Be anyone. You are the captain of this shipwrecked heart. (PAIGE gags.) I would give anything to make you happy. Please say you like me. I need you. Love, Marlin. P.S. Wanna borrow my (fill in popular singer or group) CDs?

Isn't that incredible? They went out twice. She thought he was a geek. She kept the CDs. Too bad. Marlin's a nice guy.

She whips through the letters, pulling out some here and there.

There's some doozies in here. Everybody talking about forever and everlasting, and what they really mean is a semester. Talking about love and passion—until one or the other does something wrong. I mean, come on. When are people gonna wise up? No one loves you totally and forever. (Reads a few selections.)

"I will love you forever and ever," "I don't know how I can spend another minute without you." Oh, puh-leeeze! "You're the greatest thing that's ever happened in my life." "I'll never leave you or forsake you." (Pause.) "I'll never leave you or forsake you." I don't remember this one.

She flips through the pages and reads:

> I loved you first. I loved you before you even knew who I was. I have given all for you—everything I have. I want to fill your heart with myself. My love doesn't see what you have done, only who you are. Will you think about me? I'll be waiting.

Get real. Who is this to?

Flips to the first page. Small pause.

Paige Wesley? It's to me.

She stands and begins pacing.

I don't remember anyone...no one's ever....Wait! This is a joke. It has to be. No one's ever written me a love letter. No one even knows I'm alive.

She flips through the pages.

Who wrote this? No hearts. No X's. No O's. No SWAK. What's this red stuff? Paint?

Looks closer.

It's *blood*? Somebody bled on this. Who would write such a...?

PAIGE flips to the end of the letter. Long pause.

Love, Jesus.

She sits, slowly.

BLACKOUT (freeze, then exit)

40

Over the Fence

Lawrence G. and Andrea J. Enscoe

Main Theme: The fall of humanity.
You may want to use this skit as part of a study of Genesis 3:1-24; Romans 3:23 or 5:12-17.

Characters
A: Little boy
E: Little girl
CARETAKER: Older man
BULLY: Tough young boy

Props: Boxes, crates, a seesaw, A-frame ladders, one big ladder, overalls, cap, red rag. **Optional:** Actor's blocks. Paint the park equipment in primary colors.

> *The playing area is covered with different-sized acting blocks and crates in primary colors, a seesaw and A-frame ladders. One big ladder towers above the rest. A and E enter.*

A (looking around in wonder): Wow. This park is really neat.

E: Yeah-huh. Look at all this cool stuff to jump on and stuff.

> *They begin running around, looking at things. They come to the big ladder.*

E: Wow, that's really way up. Scary, huh? We could fall.

A: I bet ya we could see everything from up there.

> *A suddenly bolts and climbs one of the small ladders.*

A: Look how high I am! Really high up! Can touch the sky almost!

E: Don't fall down, goofy head.

> *They climb all over, challenging each other, saying, "Hey, I can balance!" "Hey, I got my eyes closed!" "I'm higher!" etc.*

A: Look! I'm the topperest! (Looks out toward the audience.) Wow. I can see the fence from here. Way over there.

E: I wonder what's on the other side?

> *CARETAKER comes in, dressed in overalls and a cap with a red rag hanging out of his back pocket.*

CARETAKER: Hey, you kids havin' fun in here?

A & E: Sure, Mr. Takecare!

CARETAKER: Now you be careful up there. Don't stand on the top of that, okay? Aw, you'll be all right. Climb on anything you want. (He stops at the big ladder.) Oh, listen kids, I don't want you to climb on this one, hear me? It's way too tall. It's dangerous. That's my rule, got it? Climb it and you'll get hurt. Understand?

> *A and E nod.*

Good. That's very good. (He looks around.) Yes, you'll like this place, I think. Just holler if you need me.

> *CARETAKER goes out. A and E play awhile and end up near the big ladder. They touch it and look around, flinching.*

A: Let's play on the seesaw.

E: Yeah! (They jump on the seesaw and start moving.)

A: See anything? Can you see—

E:—Saw the fence.

A: Can you see Mr. Takecare?

E: No. Don't see him. Wonder where he is?

>   *BULLY unfolds from behind a block, leans on the big ladder.*

A: Hey, do you think Mr. Takecare's gone?

BULLY: A'course he's gone, stupidheads!

>   *A and E start with surprise.*

>   He just yells at ya then he takes off. He always does that.

A (planting his feet on the ground): Hey, who are you?

BULLY (mimicking): "Hey, who am I?" Your pal, that's who. I know this place, got it? I can show you around. Fill ya in. First you need to get a good look around. So, why'ncha climb this ladder here and take a peek.

>   *A gets off of the seesaw quickly. E crashes to the ground.*

A: Mr. Takecare told us not to.

BULLY: Aw, he just don't wan'cha seein' over the fence. That's azactly what you wanna do, isn't it? Ya see over the fence and you'll know as much about the place as he does. Come on. Ya wanna grow up smart, don'cha? You deserve to know the way'a things, don'cha? Climb on up.

E: I don't think we oughta.

BULLY: Dare ya! Double dare ya! *Quadroople eleventy billion times dare ya!*

>   *A and E look at each other, then dash to the big ladder and climb up opposite sides. BULLY bee-lines it offstage.*

A (to E): You see sumthin'?

E: Naw. Just the fence. (Looks down.) Hey, ya big fibber! You said we could...hey, where'd he go?

A: I dunno. Get down fast, we're in trouble!

>   *CARETAKER enters quietly. They start down the ladder, but see CARETAKER standing there.*

CARETAKER (sadly): Come down from there.

>   *They climb down, heads hung low.*

>   Wait there. Don't move.

E: We're sorry, Mr. Takecare.

A: Yeah, this kid come in here and told us you—

CARETAKER: Shhh.

>   *While A and E watch, CARETAKER stacks all the blocks and ladders, except the big ladder, to the side.*

A: But what're you doin'?

E: Where we goin'?

CARETAKER: Over the fence. The park is closed. Come on. (He goes out.)

A: We don't wanna go now. Wait up! Mr. Takecare! We wanna stay here! Heeey!

E (starting to cry): I don't think he's gonna let us back in here again, do you?

A: I don't wanna go over the fence. I'm...scared. I never been a'scared before. I'm a'scared of going over the fence. (They look off.) Don't think there's a playground out there.

> *They hold hands and go off.*

E: Think Mr. Takecare'll look out for us out there, too?

> *BLACKOUT (exit)*

Imagine
Judith L. Roth

Main Theme: Characteristics of the Holy Spirit.
You may want to use this skit as part of a study of John 14:16,17; Romans 5:5; or 8:15,16,26,27.

Characters
DANA: Creative writing student
MS. JENKINS: Dana's writing teacher
KELLY: Dana's friend

Props: Books, writing paraphernalia, a chair, a desk, two pencils, a working microphone, a bright directional light.

It is late at night. DANA is at center stage, slumped over a pile of books and writing paraphernalia on his desk. He appears to be asleep. The voices of MS. JENKINS and KELLY are memories.

MS. JENKINS (offstage; miked with a lot of reverb): Your assignment, should you choose to accept it—(chortles) just kidding, class. If you want to pass, you'll do this. Your assignment is to write a poem about someone or something. Your poem should present that someone or something as something else. Symbolism. Imagery. You know, all that stuff we've been talking about for so long. "My love is a rose...." That sort of thing.

MS. JENKINS' voice fades on the last line. DANA stirs restlessly.

KELLY (offstage; miked with a lot of reverb): You're going to *what?*

DANA (lifting his head off the books; patiently): I'm going to write that poem about the Holy Spirit.

KELLY (sarcastically): Roses are red, violets are blue, the Holy Spirit's like a chrysanthemum, and so are you.

DANA drops his head back on the books and groans loudly. He gets up and begins pacing.

DANA (talking to himself): Okay, okay, okay, what's the Spirit like? Faithful...like the sun coming up and going down every day...like the geyser, Old Faithful....No, I don't want to talk about a geyser. Ummmmmm...like the wind—you can't see the Spirit, but the Spirit is still powerful....

KELLY: And besides, how are you going to write about something that you can't even see?

DANA (ignoring the memory): Like the wind....I think that's been done before....Okay, what else? Faithful, powerful, invisible....

KELLY: Not only that, but aren't people going to think you're a little wacky, writing about the Holy Spirit when you don't even *have* to? This is school, man.

DANA: Quit bothering me!

DANA goes over to desk and puts head down again.

MS. JENKINS (miked, unseen): Now class, here's a for instance. Imagine the Empire State Building is a petrified dinosaur. Or that Teddy Roosevelt (voice begins to fade) is a brash elderly teddy bear. Imagine the....

DANA: Imagine the Spirit—

DANA looks up and "watches" a tiny invisible spider crawl across his books. He picks it up with a pencil, watches it drop from a web-line, catches it with another pencil.

a spider....

DANA walks the invisible spider from pencil to pencil, watching the invisible web-lines it makes. He gets up from the desk and begins to walk an imaginary tightrope.

Tightrope-walking on gossamer threads
spun from this body
Some think the threads fragile and flimsy
but I have walked for years
and never fallen   never
had the line break beneath me

Some liken the....

DANA'S voice fades out as MS. JENKINS reads. Regular lights down on DANA; up on MS. JENKINS who is reading poem to grade it. She stands at the edge of the stage and reads thoughtfully. A bright directional light is aimed low and close to DANA so that his shadow towers on the wall or backdrop. DANA continues tightrope-walking, making gestures appropriate to the poem as it is read.

MS. JENKINS: Some liken the white sticky wisps to spun sugar

but this is not candy
it is my life   and it comes from within me
an unending supply
strong enough to hold my weight
and to stop that devil-fly   cut off
his buzzing and bothering around

With him bound   I am free
This Spirit-string shelters and feeds me
and though the winds gust and I sway in the breeze
my silken lair will hold   Still
some stare at this web
and see nothing
Now   watch me

I am not balancing my life upon air[1]

Lights down on MS. JENKINS. Directional light stays on DANA's final held position.

BLACKOUT (freeze, then exit)

1. Judith L. Roth, "Imagine the Spirit a Spider's Web-Maker," *Moody Monthly* (December 1986): 63.

A Friend to Depend On

Judith L. Roth

Main Theme: Choosing friends wisely.
You may want to use this skit as part of a study of Proverbs 13:20 or 18:24.

Characters
FRANNIE: Orphan with red curly hair
DADDY BIGBUCKS: Frannie's adoptive father
PRUNEJAR: Daddy's foreign butler

Props: Wig of red curly hair, several pieces of paper, a towel to wrap as a turban. **Optional:** A turban.

FRANNIE skips onto stage, talking to herself excitedly.

FRANNIE: Oh, I can't wait, I can't wait. Daddy Bigbucks is going to let me have my own car!

FRANNIE dances around. She looks offstage.

Prunejar, hurry up!

PRUNEJAR enters gracefully wearing a turban.

PRUNEJAR: Yes, miss. I am coming.

FRANNIE (sing-song): A car, a car, I get to have a car.

She looks around.

Where's Daddy Bigbucks?

PRUNEJAR: He is coming. He had a last-minute conference with the President. Let us go onto the automobile lot.

They move a ways upstage.

FRANNIE: *Ooh!* Look at all these cars!

PRUNEJAR: Yes. I see them.

FRANNIE spies the perfect car.

FRANNIE (running over to it): Prunejar, *look. This* is my car. Isn't that the most beautiful shade of blue you ever saw? And *look.* A sunroof! Mag wheels, white leather seats, a stereo with Dolby surround sound!

She leans way in through the imaginary car's open window and squeals. She pokes her head back out.

And Prunejar! It's got a Jacuzzi in the back!

DADDY BIGBUCKS enters. FRANNIE sees him and runs to meet him.

DADDY DADDY DADDY!!!

DADDY BIGBUCKS (stoically): My dear Frannie. This is a big day in your life. We are going to pick out your very first car. Now, I have a little speech prepared for this occasion.

He pulls out several pages and shuffles them. FRANNIE grabs at his arm, trying to lead him onto the lot.

FRANNIE: *Daddy Daddy Daddy!!* Come look!

DADDY (oblivious): First I'd like to thank everyone who made this occasion possible.

>DADDY *looks around, then smiles broadly.*

>I suppose that would be me, wouldn't it?

FRANNIE (in a yoo-hoo voice): Oh Daddy Bigbucks....

DADDY: Now Frannie, I want you to think of a car as your friend.

FRANNIE (still in yoo-hoo voice): Come see my be-yoo-ti-ful ca-ar....

DADDY: You pick friends that are dependable, who will care about you, who you can trust....

FRANNIE (giving up on yoo-hooing): It's got bucket seats.

DADDY: You pick friends who will be good to you....

FRANNIE: It's got electric windows.

DADDY: Friends who won't get you in trouble....

FRANNIE: The chrome *gleams*.

DADDY: Friends that don't have wild personalities....

FRANNIE: Daddy, it has tinted windows so you have privacy in the Jacuzzi.

DADDY: *What* are you talking about?

FRANNIE: My car. I picked it out already. It called to me and I knew it was mine. Oh, Daddy, come meet Maximillian. I know you'll love him.

>She pulls DADDY BIGBUCKS *onto the lot and over to the car.*

>(To the car) Maximillian, meet Daddy Bigbucks.

DADDY: Maximillian?

FRANNIE: Isn't he precious? My very own car-car-car.

>DADDY *sticks his head through the open window.*

DADDY: Frannie, what is that large tub of water doing in the back seat?

FRANNIE: Isn't it great? Don't you just love this car? Isn't this the best car you ever saw?

>DADDY *looks around at it. Kicks a tire.*

DADDY: Well. How does it run?

FRANNIE (blankly): Run?

DADDY: You know—when you push on the gas pedal, does the car go anywhere?

FRANNIE: Oh, that. Well, I don't know yet.

>DADDY *pulls out his speech again.*

DADDY: Now Frannie, I want you to think of a car as your friend. You don't choose a friend by the color of her hair, or by how popular she is, do you? No. You choose a friend who you can trust....

FRANNIE: Yeah yeah yeah. I heard all that.

DADDY: Would you want someone for a friend that's always getting you in trouble?

FRANNIE: Well, no.

DADDY: What if this car was always breaking down far from home?

FRANNIE: But I *love* this car, Daddy.

DADDY: You might love your wild friend, too. But it wouldn't be very smart to—what's the expression you use? Hang around. It wouldn't be very smart to hang around with a wild friend, now, would it?

> *FRANNIE looks frantically around. She sees PRUNEJAR.*

FRANNIE: Prunejar! Tell Daddy what a great car this is!

PRUNEJAR: You must listen to your daddy, Miss.

DADDY: Don't be discouraged, Frannie. Just because a car is dependable doesn't mean it has to be boring. We'll have our mechanic check out, uh, Maximillian and see if he fits the bill....If not, we'll find a car that's even better.

> *DADDY puts his arm around FRANNIE and they walk towards the exit. PRUNEJAR follows.*

A car you could name Samuel. Or Abraham. That's it—we'll get you a Lincoln....

> *BLACKOUT (exit)*

Anointed with Oil

Lawrence G. and Andrea J. Enscoe

Main Theme: Caring for other Christians.
You may want to use this skit as part of a study of John 13:34,35; Acts 2:44-47 or Philippians 2:1-4.

Characters
MACHINE: (played by approximately five to ten people)
WHEEL
COG
LAST ONE IN LINE: (part of machine)
CONNIE
MACHINE PART: (part of machine)

Props: Two oil cans, a table.

> *A line of five to ten skit players—the MACHINE—are onstage acting out the movements of the "Machine" acting exercise. (This is developed by starting with one player who makes a machine-like movement. Another player builds a movement onto the machine that reacts to the first move ment, and so on.) Each plays a part of the machine—hissing, pinging and whirring toward some productive end. But there are some key parts missing. The MACHINE chugs on a few moments, though it's perfectly clear the work is hindered. The MACHINE parts frown and look around, wondering what's happening. The noises become more and more discordant and halting. COG and WHEEL enter, moving stiffly and mechanically, like rusted tin men.*

MACHINE (separate people taking separate lines): Hey, where you guys been! Nothing's gettin' done over here! We need you! Snap to! Fall in! Line up!

WHEEL (waving to machine while talking to COG out of the side of his mouth): Hey, Cog! Looks like we're in hot water again.

COG: Looks like it, Wheel. I'm movin' a little slow today. You?

WHEEL: You don't know the half of it.

> *COG and WHEEL do limber-up exercises.*

COG: Man, I need to spend more time workin' out. I'm draggin'.

WHEEL: No kidding. My joints are all—

MACHINE (together): COME ON! (Separately) You're holdin' up progress! We gotta move ahead! Time's wasting! Hurry up! Move it!

COG: Look, we need to be in shape or we're not gonna get anywhere.

WHEEL: No kidding.

> *COG and WHEEL produce oil cans and lubricate their joints. They hold up the cans, shaking them and looking inside.*

WHEEL: Hey, I didn't bring a whole lot of oil today. I think I've got just about enough left for another lube.

COG: Same here. Hey, you guys bring any extra oil in case we—?

MACHINE (together): NO! (Separately) Getting oil's your job! I've only got enough for me! I didn't bring any extra! I oil up at home! (Together) NOW GET IN LINE!

> *COG and WHEEL shrug and get in line. The MACHINE chugs along in harmony. In mime, the MACHINE parts pass something invisible down the line, over wheels, cogs, and gizmos. The LAST ONE IN LINE turns, like a pair of robotic arms, and drops the "product" on the floor, making the sound of a crash. The passing and crashing is repeated several times.*

MACHINE (with separate people taking separate lines): Hey, what's going on down there?! What's that crashing noise?! What's breakin' down? We're doin' our part over here!

LAST ONE IN LINE: I can't help it, you Bozos! Somebody's missin'!

COG: It's Connie. Connie Vayer. She's not in her place at the end. We can't finish anything without her.

> *As they speak, CONNIE VAYER walks in. She grinds forward like a toy whose batteries are running low, then stops—a little forward, then stops. Finally, near center, she halts and tips forward.*

WHEEL: Look, there she is.

CONNIE (weakly; stiff jawed): Heeelp meee.

> *The MACHINE keeps chugging away.*

MACHINE: She looks terrible. What's her problem? A couple'a quarts low, looks like to me. She should'a took care of herself at home. Yeah, I don't have anything for her.

CONNIE: Heeelp meee.

COG: We gotta help her, Wheel, or nothin'll get done.

WHEEL: Both of us don't have any extra. I've just got what I need in case I start to lose steam.

COG: How about it, everybody? Let's all oil her up and we can—

MACHINE (together): NO! THERE'S ONLY ENOUGH FOR ME!

CONNIE (barely understandable): Oiiil caaan.

COG: How 'bout it, Wheel?

WHEEL: I can't afford to break down.

COG: Neither can I, Bolthead. But if YOU give her a little, and I give her a little, we'll both pull this off. And we'll have enough for the both of us, got it?

> *WHEEL thinks a bit, then nods. They step out. Immediately The MACHINE becomes discordant. They oil CONNIE's joints. She stands, moves limbs, starts to walk. She tries to talk.*

WHEEL: What she sayin'?

COG: I think she said, "My mouth." She wants us to oil her jaw.

WHEEL: Think we could just leave that part rusty?

COG (smacking him): Oil it!

> *They oil each side of her jaw.*

CONNIE: Thanks, you sweet things, you! Wow, what a relief. Now I can just move anywhere I want. Incredible! I just can't believe you two would sacrifice some of your—

MACHINE: COME ON!

WHEEL (to COG): Told ya.

> *They all jump back in line. The MACHINE goes into harmony again. CONNIE is there to pick up the imaginary product and carry it to the table, where she is now stacking them up. For a moment, we listen to the well-oiled machinery.*

MACHINE: That's better! Now we're cookin' with gas! With oil! What a sound! Purrin' like a cat!

> *One of the MACHINE parts suddenly halts a little.*

MACHINE PART: Hey, just felt a little stiffness. In my elbows, I think. Can anybody spare a little oil? I ran out this morning.

> *Silence. COG and WHEEL look at each other. Finally....*

MACHINE (separately): I think so. Sure, I got a little extra in my back pocket. Gotcha, dude, fix ya right up. No worries around here.

MACHINE PART: Thanks.

> *COG and WHEEL look at each other and smile. The MACHINE continues purring on.*

> *BLACKOUT (freeze, then exit)*

Perfect for the Job

Lawrence G. and Andrea J. Enscoe

Main Theme: We are saved by God's grace.
You may want to use this skit as part of a study of John 3:16,17; Romans 3:22-24; Ephesians 2:8,9 or 1 Timothy 1:12-16.

Characters
COURTNEY: A job applicant
GRACE: Interviewer for the job

Props: Two chairs, papers, a clipboard, a portable file. **Optional:** A chalkboard.

> *Onstage are two chairs and a chalkboard that reads "INTERVIEWS HERE." GRACE sits shuffling through papers with a clipboard on her lap. COURTNEY VANCE comes in, dressed tweedy and carrying a file.*

COURTNEY (calling off): Through here? Oh, I see. Thanks. (She crosses to GRACE.) I'm here for the job. (Fishes out a paper.) Here's my resume. Laser-jet printed. Macintosh. (Taps the paper.) Linen–finish paper.

GRACE (smiling): Very impressive.

> *COURTNEY grins, standing there.*

Ah, you can just have a seat over there. I'll call you.

COURTNEY (a little disappointed): Oh. Fine.

> *COURTNEY sits. Notices the audience. Leans in.*

I'm not, like, trying to sound uppity or anything, but I'm a shoo-in. I'm perfect for this job. Really. I've worked hard to build up a resume like that. Took the right courses. Aced 'em all. Extra-curricular stuff. I deserve this position. It's true.

GRACE: Courtney Vance?

COURTNEY (to the audience as she goes to GRACE): Great resume, too. Laser-jet printed. Macintosh. Linen–finish paper.

GRACE: Hello, Courtney. I'm Grace. (Shakes her hand.) Please sit down.

> *COURTNEY sits. GRACE looks at the resume.*

Well, Courtney, I have to tell you, this is really an incredible resume. (COURTNEY smiles at the audience.) I don't think I've seen one better. Three point nine G.P.A. Ninety-eighth percentile on SAT scores. Captain of the debating team. Lettered in track, swimming and golf. French, Spanish, Russian and Mandarin Chinese. Church youth group leader. Honor roll all four years. Type 80 words per minute. Scholarship awards. Your parents must be very proud of you.

COURTNEY: Thank you. Yes, they are. I've made sure of it.

GRACE: I'm certain you have. Do you mind if I ask a few questions? (COURTNEY shakes her head.) Fine. (Pulls up clipboard.) Ah, can you work full-time? Forty to forty-five hours a week?

COURTNEY: Yes, I can.

GRACE: Uh-huh. (Makes a check on the application.) Nights and weekends okay? (COURTNEY nods; GRACE checks.) Do you have your own car?

COURTNEY: Yes, I do.

GRACE (checks): Any disabilities that might hinder you on the job?

COURTNEY: None.

GRACE (checks): Have you ever lied to your mother?

COURTNEY (pauses): What?

GRACE: Have you ever lied to your mother?

COURTNEY (totally lost): Well, I...might...I think I was out kind've late once...and I—

GRACE: True or false, Courtney?

COURTNEY: True! I mean...yes. I have.

GRACE: Uh-huh. (Checks.) Have you ever cheated on a test?

COURTNEY: No way! I have never, ever—!

GRACE: Never?

COURTNEY (pause): Well, once when I was in the fourth grade—

GRACE: Uh-huh. (Checks.)

COURTNEY: Wait a minute! I was only nine years old!

GRACE: Have you ever spit on your geeky little brother's tuna sandwich before giving it to him?

COURTNEY: Hold on! How'd you know I—?

GRACE: Uh-huh. (Checks.)

COURTNEY: Time out! What does that prove?

GRACE: I'm afraid you're not perfect.

COURTNEY: But I *am* perfect for the job!

GRACE: Well, according to these answers—

COURTNEY (standing): Well, then nobody's perfect! If I'm not, *nobody is!* Look, I spit on Frankie's sandwich because he flushed my Care Bear down the toilet. You can't crash me for that! This is insane! I've worked 'til I could drop! That's killer stuff you've got in front of you! I'm the creme de la creme! *Everybody says so!* (Starts to cry.) I worked so hard....Okay...fine...I'll...I'll just—

GRACE: Relax. You've got the job, Courtney.

COURTNEY: How am I going to tell my mom—(Stops.) I got the job?

GRACE: You've got the job. I never said you didn't get it.

COURTNEY (stunned): But—I thought you said—(Pause.) Well then, what did I do to deserve the job?

GRACE: Nothing. You didn't do anything.

COURTNEY: Oh. (She sits.) That's a switch.

GRACE (holding up resume): This doesn't count, understand? Nothing you ever did counts here. You're in here on my word. (GRACE tears up resume and application.) This is history. Still want the job?

COURTNEY: Let me get this straight. Am I going to have to be perfect from now on out?

GRACE: You can try. You won't be. You've got the job either way.

COURTNEY (pauses): When would you want me to start?

GRACE: Immediately.

COURTNEY (thinks, then smiles): I'm in.

> They shake hands.
>
> BLACKOUT (freeze, then exit)

53

The Alltalk Gossip Party Line

Lawrence G. and Andrea J. Enscoe

Main Theme: Gossip hurts people.

You may want to use this skit as part of a study of Proverbs 11:12,13; 16:28; James 3:3-12 or 4:11.

Characters
ANNOUNCER: Voice from a low-budget hard-sell commercial
GIRL: Gossiping teenager
GUY: Gossiping teenager

Props: Two phones, a microphone. **Optional:** Tape player and tape of ANNOUNCER'S lines.

> *GUY and GIRL each have a phone receiver to his or her ear. They are talking animatedly (not to each other), laughing and listening with intensity. All performed silently. An ANNOUNCER'S voice can be heard, on tape or from an offstage mike.*

ANNOUNCER: Hey dudes and dudettes! Are you lonely? Are you bored with your life? Are you tired of those long Saturday afternoons with only reruns of "Gilligan's Island" and watching your baby sister eat things off the floor to make your existence bearable? Pretty scary, huh? Well, join the thousands, maybe millions, who are filling in all that dead time by talking on the telephone! That's right, it's the all new Alltalk Gossip Party Line! Just call 1-900-4GOSSIP and you can spend your Saturday afternoons talking with other bored, TV-tired people with nothing better to do than talk about other people! Sure, talk about friends at church, school or even people you barely know. Everybody's fair game on the Alltalk Gossip Party Line. Let's listen in on this dudical babe as she reaps the Alltalk Gossip Party Line benefits.

GIRL: Well, it just wouldn't surprise me about her. If you're asking me, I just wouldn't doubt it, is what I'm saying. You know, with her past and all. Yeah, her past. You didn't know about her past? Yes, her past before she started coming to our church. What? Well, *I'm* certainly not going to dish any cheese on it. Ashleigh, are you doy or what? I said I'm not going to tell you about her. You're just going to have to use your imagination. Nope. Uh-uh. I won't say a...warm. No, no, no. My lips are...you're getting warmage. Ashleigh, it would be way wrong if I told—hot! Very hot! All right. But I did *not* tell you that, got it? So, with a past like that you could prob'ly get the big picture about her and you-know-who from youth group. It just wouldn't surprise me, that's all I'm saying. What? Oh, yeah, we really should pray for her, huh? Hey, while we're on the subject, let me fill you in on some other stuff we could pray for her about!

ANNOUNCER (laughing): And who said gossip can't be spiritual? And remember, don't be afraid to be vague. Letting the other party do some of the work for you is half the fun of the Alltalk Gossip Party Line! Let's listen in on this *smooooth* operator.

GUY: It was raucous, dude. Party, yeah! It was a way thumpin' party, I'm tellin' you. Hey, you know who I saw there? Mark. Dude, Mark from youth group. If you'd been there, Major Flake, you'd'a seen him. We're talking he was wastoid. Yeah. No doubt. He asked me not to tell anyone 'cuz he was ashamed of himself, so don't tell too many people, huh? What a geek. Dude, check it out, you-know-who was there. No, older. The one from college-and-career group. Yeah, well we talked. What do you mean what else happened? Jealousy, dude. How do you know somethin' happened? (Smiles.) Yeah, well you're right about that. I am pretty killer. Well, you just let your imagination run wild. Dude, you're gonna think what you want to anyways.

ANNOUNCER: Oh, don't let the facts stop you on the Alltalk Gossip Party Line. That's half the fun of it all! Besides, get enough people on your side, and it becomes the truth anyway! So don't be in the dark anymore about what's going on outside your living room. Call the Alltalk Gossip Party Line today.

GUY/GIRL (together): Nuh-uh! That's what his second cousin's brother said. I swear!

ANNOUNCER: Start taking charge of your life—and everybody else's. Call the Alltalk Gossip Party Line today! Ninety cents for the first three minutes, two bits off of someone's reputation for every minute afterwards. So call 1-900-4GOSSIP. That's 1-900-4-G-O-S-S-I-P. Remember, it's not the truth, it's just all talk on the Alltalk Gossip Party Line!

BLACKOUT (freeze, then exit)

The Opera Wimpy Show

Lawrence G. and Andrea J. Enscoe

Main Theme: God helps us change.

You may want to use this skit as part of a study of Romans 12:2; 1 Corinthians 10:13; 2 Corinthians 3:17,18; 5:17 or Philippians 4:13.

Characters
ANNOUNCER: For television show
OPERA WIMPY: A talk show host
JIM HAZELNUT: A man in the studio audience
SOMEONE IN THE AUDIENCE
CHERYL NADA: A woman in the studio audience
SUSAN GUNNERSMA: A woman in the studio audience
MICHAEL CLEANBILL: A man in the studio audience

Props: A microphone, a candy wrapper, index cards, a candy bar, army fatigues, a large box of chocolates.
   Optional: Assorted vegetables.

ANNOUNCER (offstage): And now, live from Warmwater, Illinois, please welcome TV's most-loved talk show host—Opera Wimpy!

OPERA WIMPY enters carrying a microphone and index cards.

OPERA (into microphone): Welcome to the Opera Wimpy show. "Be not conformed to this world but be transformed by the renewing of your mind." A tall order. God's order. A big question. Just how do we change our lives? Often we get caught up in behaviors and life-styles we simply don't want to be part of anymore. Well, today we're going to talk about how to make changes in our lives by tackling one of my favorite topics—food. More importantly...chocolate. Any chocolate lovers in the audience? Well, let's meet some recovering chocoholics to see just how they changed their own lives. Jim Hazelnut, where are you?

JIM (standing; shaky and nervous. He digs through his pockets as he speaks.): Here, Opera.

OPERA goes to him, mike outstretched.

Hi, my name's Jim, and I'm a chocoholic.

OPERA: This chocolate thing. A tough nut to crack. How'd ya do it?

JIM: Well, Opera, I was in big truffle...trouble! I sat in my home out in caramel—Carmel! Shoveling in the cho...cho...cho....

OPERA: Chocolate.

JIM: Chocolate! I had to have it. Night and day. Dark, milk, semi-sweet, bittersweet. It didn't matter. When I couldn't get the real thing, I'd eat baker's ch-ch-chocolate. At work my friends'd Snicker—laugh—at me when I'd make my Mounds—rounds!—with a Baby Ruth in one hand and a Butterfinger in the other. I started developing nervous Twix—tics!—when I couldn't get any choco...choco...that stuff! Then one day, I was at home with candy wrappers all around me and I knew it was time to watch my M & M's—ps and qs. So I quit. Just like that! I just said no. It was a miracle. Now I don't even crave ch-ch-ch-

OPERA: Chocolate.

JIM: YES! I no longer need it. Not at all. Uh-uh. No way.

OPERA: Incredible. You did this on your own? Sheer will power?

JIM: Told myself I didn't want it. And I don't. I don't care if I ever see the stuff again. Told my mind that I didn't...didn't...want....(He has found an old candy wrapper in his pocket and he starts to lick the paper, ravenously.) Don't want it! Don't even think about it! (OPERA reaches for the wrapper) *Touch it and die, Wimpy!*

OPERA (pulling back): Well, let's just talk to Cheryl Nada. Cheryl are you here? Cheryl? Cheryl?

> *SOMEONE IN THE AUDIENCE is forcing CHERYL to stand: "She's right here! Over here!"*

CHERYL: I am not! Am not! No one's calling me—(Turns and sees OPERA and her mike.) Oh. Hi, Opera. How are you?

OPERA: Just fine, Cheryl. (Looks at index card.) Chocolate. Ruler of your life. Filled your head night and day. You beat it. How?

CHERYL: I never ate chocolate. Who told you that? Nuh-uh.

OPERA: You told us. On this card. Major chocoholic.

CHERYL: Oh...well, yes. I had a little problem. (She pulls out a candy bar and begins to peel the wrapper.) I used to have trouble with chocolate, but not anymore. I don't even think about chocolate. I never even see chocolate. Completely gone out've my life. Where is it? I don't know!

OPERA (staring at the bar): Really.

CHERYL: History. (Holds up the bar.) Hey, want some of this banana?

OPERA: Maybe a little denial here.

CHERYL: Hunh-uh! Get out! Fibber!

OPERA: Right. Ah...Susan Gunnersma?

SUSAN (standing and snapping to): Present, sir! (SUSAN is dressed in fatigues and has vegetables sticking out of every pocket. She eats vegetables as she speaks.)

OPERA: Susan. Portrait of a Cocoa-Bean Hound. What's your story?

SUSAN: Met with some chocolate resistance, sir! Assessed the strength of the enemy, sir! Ascertained the need for reinforcement, sir! Went to the Hagelschlag School of Chocolate Warfare in Oak Park, Illinois, sir!

OPERA: How did that help change your destructive eating patterns?

SUSAN: Adopted new behavior patterns, sir! Rise at 0500, exercise, eat carrots, oats, tofu eggs. More exercise. Self-help reading period. Lunch: salad, lentil stew and 37-grain bread. Laps, shopping maneuvers. Read *Vegetarian Times*, *Self Reliance* and *Your Chakra Is Too Small* magazines. Dinner: soy burger, tofu potatoes, watercress. Lights out, 2100 hours. (Starts jumping jacks.)

OPERA: With a schedule like that, there's no time for chocolate.

SUSAN: Sir, yes, SIR!

OPERA: All right. We've got will power, denial and behavioral modification. Let's talk a minute to Michael Cleanbill.

MICHAEL (stands with a pound-box of chocolates): Here, Opera.

OPERA: Well, aren't you brave? A box of chocolates. Tell us.

MICHAEL: It was hard. Really hard. I was way overweight and it was getting embarrassing. I knew I couldn't stop eating chocolate, so I started telling Jesus that. Told Him He had more power than I did. Then I started to realize I ate chocolate because I was angry. I wanted someone, something, to care about me. But this box of chocolates didn't love me. I had to let God love me. Then I could start loving myself. After awhile, I just started losing interest in the stuff.

OPERA: That easy?

MICHAEL: No, not easy. But lasting. You wanna chocolate, Opera?

OPERA: Oh, no, thanks. I'm on a diet. Well, maybe...just one.

> *She reaches out and takes one, as does MICHAEL. They take a nibble and chew, smiling.*
>
> *BLACKOUT (freeze, then exit)*

Best Friends
Robin Jones Gunn

Main Theme: Submitting to Jesus.
You may want to use this skit as part of a study of John 14:15,23-24; Romans 8:7-9; Philippians 2:9-11 or James 4:7.

Characters
MARCI: A Christian teenager
JESSICA: Marci's non-Christian friend

Props: Two purses, assorted shopping bags.

MARCI and JESSICA come out of a store holding shopping bags.

JESSICA (checking for her purse): Oh no! I left my purse in there!

She sees something across the way and squeals quietly.

There he is! I can't believe it! He's here!

MARCI (looking around): Who?

JESSICA (pointing in a concealed way): Danny. Marci, don't let him out of your sight! I'll be right back.

JESSICA exits quickly. MARCI starts moving furtively toward where JESSICA pointed out Danny. She bumps into an invisible Someone.

MARCI (tensely): Aauugh! (She shushes herself and looks to see who surprised her.) Oh, it's you. Don't *do* that, Jesus. You scared me to death. What are you doing here, anyway? I mean, this isn't your usual hang-out, is it?

MARCI listens for a moment and looks kind of ashamed.

Yeah, I know we were supposed to spend some time together, and we will. Really. Just as soon as I get home. But I'm with Jessica right now. You want me to witness to my friends, don't you? So that means I've gotta spend time with her. Jessica *is* my best friend, you know.

MARCI listens again and gets a determined look on her face.

No, Jesus, that just wouldn't work. You don't really want to come this time, anyway. You'd be bored, trust me. You'd be better off going back home. (She looks around.) Oh, hush. Here comes Jess.

JESSICA (tearing out of the store, waving purse): I got it! Is he still there?

MARCI (uneasily, blocking the spot where Jesus is standing): Who?

JESSICA: Danny. Oh, there he is. Hey, he's going into that movie. Come on, Marci! This is the chance I've been waiting for.

MARCI (looking uncomfortably at Jesus): Uh, wait a minute. I'm not sure I want to see that movie. I heard it has some parts in it that aren't very good, if you know what I mean. Besides, I used up all my money.

JESSICA: Hey, no problem. I'll pay. *Any*thing to get near to Danny. Just close your eyes during the parts that bother you. Come on, Marce. You know I'd go with you if it was a guy that you liked.

MARCI: Oh, all right. (She glances toward Jesus then back to JESSICA.) You go ahead and get in line to buy the tickets. I'll be right there.

JESSICA: Hurry, okay?

MARCI: I will, I will.

> *JESSICA exits.*

MARCI (to Jesus): Okay, listen. I'm going with Jessica. I'll be back before you miss me and I promise I'll close my eyes during the bad parts, okay?

> *MARCI listens and begins shaking her head.*

No, you can't come in with us. You don't understand. This really is not your kind of movie.

> *MARCI listens again, feigning patience.*

Yes, I know you wanted to meet Jessica, but I don't think this is the right time. I'll introduce you guys later, okay?

> *MARCI listens again, no longer even trying to be patient.*

I don't know when! Sometime, okay? For now, I just want to go with her and show her that I'm her friend. Now you stay here and I'll be back later.

> *MARCI heads towards the movie. Near the place where she would exit she turns around abruptly.*

Why are you following me? Don't you understand? I don't want you to come with me!

> *BLACKOUT (exit)*

Batter Up
Judith L. Roth

Main Theme: Encouraging other Christians.
You may want to use this skit as part of a study of Proverbs 16:24; Ephesians 4:29 or 1 Thessalonians 5:11.

Characters
DARREN: Little League player
KYLE: Player on Darren's team
UMPIRE
OTHER PLAYERS

Props: A bat.

> *DARREN is up to bat, as if the pitches are coming from the audience. He appears to be nervous.*

PLAYERS (from front row): Hey batter, hey batter, ay batteraybatteraybatter....

> *PLAYERS begin to call out various insults, such as, "Move in, everybody. He can't hit." DARREN swings.*

UMPIRE: Strike!

> *KYLE enters from side at DARREN's back and stays near the far end of the stage..*

KYLE (much louder than PLAYERS): Hey stupid! You couldn't hit a barn with the side of an elephant.

DARREN (whipping around): *Hey.* I thought you were on *my* team.

KYLE: I am, idiot. So don't miss next time.

> *DARREN, miffed, resumes his stance.*

You've got the stupidest way of standing I've ever seen.

DARREN: Quit talking to me. I gotta concentrate.

KYLE: Concentrate with what? Your hat size should be negative nine, since your brain is absent, and all.

> *DARREN, frustrated, holds up his bat, ready for the pitch.*

Hey, you think if you hold the bat like that, the ball will hit it?

DARREN (turning to KYLE): Come on, give me a break. I'm gonna miss the ball for sure if you keep capping on me.

> *There is a moment of silence while DARREN glares in KYLE's direction. As soon as DARREN resumes his stance, KYLE starts up again.*

KYLE: What a wimp!

UMPIRE: Strike!

DARREN: Now see what you made me do!

KYLE: Well, don't get all huffy. Temper, temper!

> *DARREN attempts to ignore KYLE.*

Maybe you should take a class on controlling that anger. And take a batting class at the same time.

DARREN visibly restrains himself from reacting to KYLE.

You batting bozo.

DARREN (putting bat down; to pitcher): Excuse me a moment. (To KYLE.) Can I talk to you, please?

KYLE (amiable): Sure, loser.

DARREN: If I miss this pitch, we lose the game. Does that mean anything to you?

KYLE: Sure. It means you're gonna lose the game for us. Nice going, lamebrain.

DARREN (with forced patience): I don't have to miss the pitch. It might help if you cheered for me instead of against me.

KYLE: Nah.

DARREN: You don't mind losing?

KYLE: Why should I care? It's gonna be your fault.

DARREN: It's still your team. And your dad's watching. And the whole neighborhood's watching. What's with you, anyhow?

UMPIRE: Batter up!

DARREN resumes batting stance. Pause.

KYLE (sarcastically): Well, if you really want to know, seeing you foul up is more fun than winning, *any* day.

DARREN grits his teeth and keeps his position. Pause.

You're basically slime.

DARREN (swinging his bat wildly): Aaaaaaaugh!

UMPIRE: Strike three! You're out!

DARREN spins to a stop. Looks dejectedly at his bat.

KYLE: Told ya you'd miss.

BLACKOUT (freeze, then exit)

Whoever Wrote 1 Corinthians 13:4 Didn't Have a Sister Like Zanny

Lawrence G. and Andrea J. Enscoe

Main Theme: Love is patient and kind.
You may want to use this skit as part of a study of 1 Corinthians 13:4; Ephesians 4:2 or Colossians 3:12.

Characters
ROBIN: Teenage girl
ZANNY: Robin's nine-year-old sister

Props: A chair, five to ten stuffed animals, a Bible, a jeans skirt.

ROBIN sits in a chair, stuffed animals on her lap and all around her. An open Bible lies at her feet.

ROBIN: I'm just reading some verses we're supposed to talk about in Youth Group and I run across this—1 Corinthians 13:4. "Love is patient, love is kind. It does not envy...." I mean, come on! this flips my switch, I gotta tell ya. I'm saying to myself, "Robin, this is impossible," know what I mean? Oh, not because I can't love anyone. I mean, it's not that I'm not patient and kind, y'know? It's just that, well, I'll give it to ya straight. I got a little sister. (Small pause.) Her name is Zanny. (Looks up.) *Patient?* Why did'ya have to put *that* in there? (Looks back at audience.) God's got a Son, but it's obvious He does *not* have a little sister. (She stops.) Okay, I have to try this out. This is gonna take practice. And if I practice with Zanny, she'll think I'm going soft on her and then life, as I know it, will be over

ROBIN leans down and picks up two stuffed animals. It's the "Zanny and Robin Puppet Hour. She uses a stuffed animal to represent each of them, playing out the lines using the animals like puppets.

ZANNY VOICE (a whiny, irritating voice): Hey, Robin. Mark Johnson called.

ROBIN: When?! When did he call?!

ZANNY VOICE: Oh, two weeks ago.

ROBIN (under her breath): "Love is patient....Love is patient." What did Mark say, O Little Sister of Mine?

ZANNY VOICE: He wanted to ask you out—

ROBIN: What?! He noticed me?!

ZANNY VOICE: I told him you already had a date with Myron Snively. Well, you did, yeah huh, you did!

ROBIN (under breath): "Love is patient." Yes, you told the truth, Zanny. I'm proud of you. Did he say he'd call back?

ZANNY VOICE: He said he'd call this week t'ask you out for ice cream.

ROBIN: Really?!

ZANNY VOICE: I told him to forget it. I told him you thought you were a fat cow and that you were on this, like, massive diet—

ROBIN: AHHHHHHHH!

Her "Robin" animal pounces on "Zanny," works her over and drop kicks her into the audience.

Let's try "Love is kind," shall we? (She gets another "Zanny" animal.) Hey, Zanny Banany, what's the deal? You look awfully sad. Did you flunk fingerpainting again?

ZANNY VOICE: Oh, Robin Bobbinhead. I feel so bad. I really do.

ROBIN: Why, little Zanny?

ZANNY VOICE: Well, I accidentally taped over your Richard Marx videos with *The Wonderful World of Disney*.

ROBIN: AHHHHH! (ROBIN drop kicks "Zanny" into the audience.) Well, that was a massive failure. All right. One more try. "Love does not envy." (ROBIN picks up another "Zanny" animal.) Hey, Zanny Fanny, why d'ya look so happy? You're grinning from ear to pierced-long-before-I-was-ever-allowed-to ear.

ZANNY VOICE: Mom and Dad just said I could have a '66 Mustang on my 16th birthday.

ROBIN (under her breath): "Love is not envious," "Love is not envious." Why'd they tell you that, you little...kid.

ZANNY VOICE: They said they loved me, and that I shouldn't be deprived of some radical transportation. (ROBIN is now snorting.) And besides, they didn't want me buggin' 'em for the car keys every five minutes like you—

ROBIN: AHHHHHH! (Jumps on "Zanny," bops her on the head and then drop kicks her.) You little slime! I always wanted a car! But nooooo! You think I like asking for the car keys every five minutes you buck-toothed little...(notices the audience)...A little envy there? Uh-huh, just a tad bit. (She dumps the animals.) This just won't work. I'm like...addicted to wailing on her. What am I going to do? Zanny expects it from me. (A knock.) Yeah?

ZANNY (offstage): Can I come in?

ROBIN: Stay out.

> *ZANNY comes in.*

ZANNY: You know your radical new jeans skirt? The one mom said fit too tight in the rear because you keep buying size 7/8 when you should be buying 9/10's?

ROBIN (patiently): Yes, Zanny.

ZANNY (holds the skirt up): I just spilled Nestle's Quik on it.

> *ROBIN stifles a scream. She picks up a stuffed animal and drop kicks it. Then she turns around to ZANNY.*

ROBIN (with infinite patience): What happened, Zanny?

ZANNY (as they go out): See, I was showing Ginah what a cool skirt it was 'n how I wanted one an' that's how it happened.

ROBIN: Let's see if Mom knows how to get the stain out.

ZANNY: I'm really sorry! What a geek! I was just showin' it to Ginah. Honest!

ROBIN: I know you didn't mean it. We'll work on it. (Pause.) By the way, Zanny, have Mom and Dad said anything to you about a '66 Mustang?

> *BLACKOUT (exit)*

A Tangy Talk

David Swaney

Main Theme: Accepting each other.
You may want to use this skit as part of a study of Acts 10:34,35; Romans 15:7 or Galatians 3:28.

Characters
FRED: A banana
TED: A tangerine
ED: A lime
RED: A Reese's Peanut Butter Cup

Props: A board game, pizza, four glasses, a fork. Optional: Food costumes—a banana, a tangerine, a lime, a Reese's Peanut Butter Cup.

> *FRED, RED, TED and ED, dressed in their respective food costumes, are seated at a kitchen table in a messy bachelorish-looking apartment. They are playing a board game and eating pizza. RED and ED are on one side, FRED and TED are on the other. ED and TED directly face each other.*

FRED: I just got sick of her calls and her letters and her pestering. So I told her off. I said, "Mom, you've got to let me lead my own life now. Butt out."

ED: Way to go. Hang tough.

RED: Yeah, be strong.

TED: Assertive.

TED, RED, ED: And *studly!*

> *All three clink glasses together. Players turn their attention to the game for a moment. FRED rolls and moves his marker.*

TED (looking at window behind FRED): It's Bonzo, Fred! Run for it!

FRED: Aauugh! (FRED jumps and whirls around to look at window.) Cut that out! (He sits down.) I've dreamt about that for four nights in a row, now. Every night it's the same. He captures me, pours a bowl of Frosted Flakes and milk, reaches for a knife, and then everything goes black.

ED: Maybe it's the sardine and pickle pizza.

FRED: I doubt it. (He takes a bite of pizza.)

ED: I think I'll have another slice. (Reaches for pizza.)

FRED (rapping ED's knuckles with a fork): Not quite. The rest is mine. You've had enough for an Ed.

ED: Ned? I'm not—

FRED: *Ed.*

ED: Oh.

TED: Speaking of Ned....

RED: When?

TED: Just now.

RED: Oh.

TED: Anyhow....How *is* Ned?

FRED: I saw him at the mall last week. He's...

TED: What?

FRED: Changed. He has hair down to his shoulders, and some of it's blue, and some pink, and I think some green.

ED: Did you talk to him?

FRED: No. I was shopping for a Langstrom 7-inch gangly wrench with my girlfriend, and she already thinks I'm weird.

TED: I can't imagine why.

ED: Did he see you?

FRED: Yeah, he sort of waved, but I pretended I didn't see.

ED: You nob. What a yellow streak.

TED: Fred, would you agree with Kant, that rational creatures have inherent worth, solely because of their possession of rationality?

FRED: Well, that sounds good—

ED: Or that acting morally is using principles you believe everyone ought to live up to?

FRED: I guess so—

TED: Mill said that tyranny of the majority is one of the greatest problems in modern democracies.

RED: Yeah, like, one time I saw this "Diff'rent Strokes" show where Arnold gets put in a hospital room with this white girl, and her dad gets all mad just 'cause Arnold's black, so Arnold and the girl run away....

> *RED stops, noticing blank stares from the other three.*

ED: What an intellectual quasar, Red.

RED: Oh, you guys think you're so hot.

TED: OK, what's normative ethics?

ED: Or Hume's basic tenets?

TED: Explain existentialism.

ED: And the pragmatic method.

TED: Go on.

> *TED whistles "Jeopardy" theme. After a few seconds, TED and ED look at each other, cross arms into X's in front of their bodies and simultaneously make a buzzer sound.*

FRED: Ted and Ed, you're doing the exact same thing you just talked about. Isn't Red included in that statement about rational creatures?

66

ED: Well, I guess so.

FRED: Just because Red is ignorant in some areas you are well-versed in doesn't mean you can attack him to feel superior.

TED (dejectedly): Gosh.

FRED: Now what do you have to say to Red?

TED and ED (with heads hanging): Sorry.

FRED: I have my own quote—"This is my command. Love each other"—That's from Jesus. I think that sums it up pretty well. If you have a genuine love for someone you'll try to make them feel good about themselves. Isn't that what we all want?

ED (ashamed): Yeah.

> *RED rolls dice, moves his marker and takes a card.*

FRED: Does anyone have anything else to say?

RED (waving the card): Yeah. I just won second prize in a beauty contest. (RED puts his hand out to FRED.) Pay me ten bucks.

> *BLACKOUT (freeze, then exit)*

Butterflies Are Insects, Too

Judith L. Roth

Main Theme: Accepting each other.

You may want to use this skit as part of a study of Acts 10:34,35; Romans 15:7; Galatians 3:28 or Philippians 2:3,4.

Characters
CHRISTIE: A junior high girl
EVERETT: Christie's dad

Props: A comfortable chair, a book, a butterfly costume with antenna. **Optional**: Junk food.

> *CHRISTIE is sprawled on a chair, reading a book and eating junk food. EVERETT, dressed in a butterfly costume, walks past CHRISTIE, trying to get her attention.*

EVERETT: Christie, have you seen my antenna?

CHRISTIE (not looking up): Your what?

EVERETT: You know, my feelers. My antenna. The things that belong on my head.

CHRISTIE (looking up without expression): They're on your head, Dad. (She goes back to reading.)

EVERETT (feeling his head): Oh, so they are.

> *EVERETT looks at CHRISTIE reading.*

Well? Aren't you going to comment on my outfit?

CHRISTIE: Okay. Aren't you a little chunky to be wearing such tight-fitting clothes?

EVERETT (sighing; sits down): You're not in the mood for a fun-filled chat today, are you?

CHRISTIE: It's just that I know what you're going to say. I'm not sure how you're going to tie it in with that costume, but it's about Janet, right?

EVERETT: Yeah, it's about your cousin. Too obvious?

CHRISTIE: I'm beginning to see the pattern. Monkey suits for political lectures. Mr. Clean costumes for anything having to do with my room. And for some reason, you wear insect outfits when you're making a point about someone my own age.

EVERETT: Wow. I didn't even know I had a pattern.

CHRISTIE: You're creative, Dad. But not too subtle.

EVERETT: Okay. Next time I'll try and surprise you. But as long as I'm in this outfit, we might as well talk.

CHRISTIE: Wait. Let me guess the connection. Janet is like a butterfly. Right now she's just a caterpillar, but someday she'll blossom into a beautiful butterfly and I won't be ashamed to be seen with her.

EVERETT: Come on. How cliche can you get? Now sit up and pay attention to your old dad.

> *EVERETT reaches behind him for something invisible, holds it in his shut hand and goes toward CHRISTIE.*

Here. I have something for you.

> *EVERETT puts his hand out, still shut, to CHRISTIE, who holds her hand out expectantly.*

It's a cockroach.

CHRISTIE screams, jerks back her hand and clambers up onto her chair as far away from EVERETT as she can get. She puts her hands over her mouth to muffle her screams. EVERETT opens his hand to show her his empty hand.

Just kidding!

CHRISTIE: Dad! How could you do that?

EVERETT: Well, the costume wasn't going over so well. I thought I'd better spice it up a bit.

CHRISTIE: Okay. You got my attention. What's the point?

EVERETT: The point is, you hate bugs. I mean, you weren't jumping around on that chair for nothing. You really hate the little boogers.

CHRISTIE: Yes. I do. And don't you ever pull anything like that again.

EVERETT (holding out his wings): I am a bug, but you don't hate me, do you?

CHRISTIE: This isn't a real good time to ask that question, Dad.

EVERETT: Let me rephrase that. You like butterflies, even though they're bugs.

CHRISTIE: That's different. Butterflies are pretty, not icky.

EVERETT: Ever see a butterfly without its wings?

CHRISTIE: Dad! That's gross!

EVERETT: No, now think about it. Butterflies have these dark skinny bug bodies with a bunch of spindly legs that kind of wave around...and antennae on their heads, and bug eyes. Ooo, that *is* kind of gross.

CHRISTIE: Bleah. Now I'll never enjoy a butterfly again.

EVERETT (with a disgusted look on his face): Where was I going with this?

CHRISTIE: Something about Janet.

EVERETT (thinking): Janet. Let's try it this way. You don't like Janet because she's fat and she only wears one earring in each ear and her clothes are out of it.

CHRISTIE: Don't make me sound so shallow. There's more than that. I mean, she likes *Barry Manilow.*

EVERETT (sarcastically): Okay, I admit there're a lot of negatives. But there's a lot of good things about your cousin, too. I think Janet is like a butterfly, but you're so busy looking at her gross bug parts that you don't see any of her beautiful parts.

CHRISTIE: You sound like Mister Rogers or somebody.

EVERETT: I was hoping my visual aids would make it sound not so corny.

CHRISTY: Dad. You're wearing a butterfly costume and you're trying not to be corny?

EVERETT: Okay, okay, the costumes don't work anymore. Next time I'll do a music video. Just think about it, will you, Christie? You're a nice girl, and Janet is your very own cousin. I think God would be happy to see you looking past Janet's appearance and her Barry Manilow records.

CHRISTIE (sheepishly): Oh, yeah. God.

EVERETT: Accepts you just the way you are.

CHRISTIE (play-acting Mister Rogers): Can you say "acceptance?"

EVERETT and CHRISTIE (together, still imitating): Sure you can!

They start laughing and EVERETT bonks CHRISTIE on the head with one of his wings.

BLACKOUT (freeze, then exit)

The Best Deal in the World

Jim and Lisa Suth

Main Theme: Eternal life in Christ.

You may want to use this skit as part of a study of John 6:25-58; Romans 6:23 or 1 John 5:11,12.

Characters
SALESMAN
YOUNG MAN

Props: A loud jacket and clashing pants, a Bible, a contract, a pen. **Optional:** Signs with slogans as labeled below, a huge toy pencil.

> *SALESMAN, dressed in a very loud jacket with clashing pants, is pacing around the floor of a large showroom. Signs cover the room with slogans like: "Why More People Choose the World," "Easy Credit Terms," "What Makes the World So Affordable?" etc. The SALESMAN is obviously only interested in a sale. A YOUNG MAN carrying a Bible enters the showroom and wanders around aimlessly.*

SALESMAN: Can I help you?

YOUNG MAN: No....I'm just looking.

SALESMAN (mocking): I'm glad you told me that. I'll help you find it.

YOUNG MAN: Find what?

SALESMAN: Well, whatever you're looking for, of course.

YOUNG MAN (confused): What am I looking for? Oh yeah....Eternal life.

SALESMAN: You mean the good life.

YOUNG MAN: No, eternal life. I was just next door and the guy over there had this great deal. I can get guaranteed eternal life if I just turn my life over to Christ. (He opens the Bible and points inside.) The brochure says there's no down payment or anything, but I thought before I make a big decision like that I'd better shop around. What kind of deal can you give me?

SALESMAN: Well, you're in the right place, my boy. I'm glad you decided to shop around. I've got the best deal in the world.

YOUNG MAN: On eternal life? That's great!

SALESMAN (leaning against object in an attempt to be cool): What color did you want? Basic black, passionate purple, neon orange, or my personal favorite: hot-as-hell red.

YOUNG MAN: Wow! Color choices! All I could get at that other place was white.

SALESMAN: I didn't even tell you how many shades of grey we have. That's another big favorite.

YOUNG MAN: So what's all this gonna cost me?

SALESMAN (aside to audience): I love this part. (With great showmanship; to YOUNG MAN.) Why that's the greatest thing about the world, my friend. It's absolutely free!

YOUNG MAN: Impossible. There's no such thing as a free lunch. It's gotta cost me something.

SALESMAN: Nope. Nothing.

YOUNG MAN: You're lying.

SALESMAN: Would I lie to you? (Short pause.) Don't answer that, Son, just step in here and let the contract speak for itself. (They move back to the office.) Have a seat.

YOUNG MAN: Thanks. (He starts patting his pockets.) Now, where did I put those glasses?

SALESMAN: Glasses?! (He holds out the contract.) Pal, just put your John Hancock down there at the bottom. (Offers huge toy pencil.) That's enough for us. We *know* where you live.

YOUNG MAN (feeling pushed): Well, at least let me look it over?

SALESMAN: Ah...it's just your standard run-of-the-mill contract. We can work out the details later. Just sign it. There's a line forming outside. The world's pretty popular these days.

YOUNG MAN (reading quickly through the contract): Wait a minute! What's this clause about reaping and sowing? You mean I may actually have to suffer the consequences of my actions?

SALESMAN: Oh, just ignore that part. How often does that happen, anyway? Skip down to paragraph three. Read about the fun times with all the money and friends you get. The world has a lot to offer, you know.

YOUNG MAN: Yeah, but for how long? It says here that the wages of sin is death.

SALESMAN: Well....As you travel the road of life there are bound to be a few little problems here or there.

YOUNG MAN (beginning to see through the SALESMAN's talk): Hey, when we're talking about eternal life, death is a big problem.

SALESMAN (getting rattled): Boy, you *are* picky, aren't you?

YOUNG MAN: I have a right to be picky. It's my life we're talking about. And look at this eternal damnation clause. I'd be nuts if I signed this.

SALESMAN: Look. Obviously you and I got started off on the wrong foot. (Leaning forward secretively.) Listen. You seem like a pretty sharp guy, and I wouldn't do this for just anybody, but....If you sign today, I'll throw in the reincarnation package for nothing. That way if it doesn't work out the first time, you can always come back as an ostrich. Or maybe a cow.

YOUNG MAN: A cow?!

SALESMAN: Hey, don't knock it. In some places, that's quite an honor

YOUNG MAN: I want to do this right the first time. As *me*.

SALESMAN (losing patience): Who's fooling who, Buddy? Everybody is eventually going to die.

YOUNG MAN: Oh, I know that. I'm just concerned about where I'll end up.

> The YOUNG MAN is convinced he doesn't want to buy. He stands to go.

Thank you for your time.

SALESMAN: Wait. *Wait!* You're passing up the deal of a lifetime. The world could be gone tomorrow.

YOUNG MAN (with a short sober pause): I know. That's what I'm worried about.

> *YOUNG MAN exits.*

SALESMAN: Man, that's the second one today. I should have told him about the rebate.

> *SALESMAN suddenly brightens up as he looks offstage. Talks while exiting.*

Oh, hi! Come on in. I've got the best deal in the world.

> *BLACKOUT (exit)*

The Very Least
Lawrence G. and Andrea J. Enscoe

Main Theme: Helping the needy.

You may want to use this skit as part of a study of Matthew 25:34-46; Luke 14:12-14; Acts 20:35 or Hebrews 13:16.

Characters
NEEDYDUDE
PREACH
CAL Q. LATOR
DOE NATION

Props: A chair (substitute for the acting block), a jacket covered with Christian buttons, a muffler, a stocking cap, a Bible, a business suit, an umbrella, a checkbook, a small calculator, a wallet, an offering can that reads, "God Cares," wallet pictures, cash. **Optional:** A black acting block, sound effects of street sounds, a drum, glasses.

The playing area is empty, except for a black acting block. We hear the sounds of a busy street, then softly a drum beat begins to beat at a steady cadence (this will build during the scene).

NEEDYDUDE comes in, looking around. He is wearing dirty, baggy clothes and looks disheveled. He sits on the block, tired, hungry and dejected. He shivers from the cold.

PREACH enters and falls into a circular march around the block in rhythm with the drumbeat. He is wearing a jacket with lots of Christian buttons, sayings and symbols pinned to it. He's also wearing a warm muffler and stocking cap. He reads from a huge black Bible and is preaching, mouth going and finger pointing. We watch him for a moment.

The streets sounds fade out.

NEEDYDUDE sees PREACH and is delighted. He comes up and pulls out his pockets, then holds a hand out. PREACH brushes past him roughly. NEEDYDUDE spins and falls to the floor. He gets up and goes to PREACH shivering and holding his hand out, asking for the muffler or cap. He gets knocked down again as PREACH pushes by him.

CAL Q. LATOR comes in next. He is wearing a business suit and glasses. He has an umbrella under his arm and is balancing his checkbook with a small hand-held calculator. CAL falls in step with PREACH.

NEEDYDUDE smiles and stands. He shows his pockets to CAL and shows an empty wallet, watching a moth fly out of it. He holds out a hand. CAL brushes past and NEEDYDUDE spins and topples to the floor, as before.

DOE NATION comes in, dressed officiously and carrying an offering can that reads, "God cares." She falls in step around the circle with the other two.

NEEDYDUDE stands. He reads the can. He smiles and claps and goes to her, pointing to his pockets and holding out his hand. She knocks into him without noticing and he tumbles to the floor.

NEEDYDUDE stands, upset. He brushes himself off. Suddenly, he feels a hunger pang and stoops over a moment. He shivers. He turns and goes to the three goose-stepping in cadence, faster and faster. He moves between all three, holding out a hand, pointing to his wallet and his pockets. He mimes cradling a baby. He shows pictures. All the while he's dodging them as they pace toward him oblivious of his presence. He kneels to beg from them, but they bear down on him and he scrambles continually out of the way of one and into the path of another. Finally, he escapes.

NEEDYDUDE stands on the block. He waves for their attention. No go. He jumps up and down. He does a little dance. He pretends like he's hanging himself. No response. CAL Q. LATOR drops his umbrella and NEEDYDUDE gets down to pick it up. He holds the umbrella up to give it to CAL. CAL sees the umbrella and thinks he's being held up. He steps out of line and waves at the others. They don't notice. NEEDYDUDE points at the umbrella and shakes his head—it's not a mugging. CAL pulls out his wallet and takes out money. He holds it out to NEEDYDUDE, who is still shaking his head no. As they stand there, DOE comes by and snatches it, stuffing it into her can. CAL looks at DOE, then at NEEDYDUDE, who opens the umbrella and does a little Fred Astaire dance. CAL blusters, smacks NEEDYDUDE over the head with the wallet and gets back in step.

NEEDYDUDE drops the umbrella and rubs his head. He gets into the center of the circle and watches them all go by. He has a hunger pang. It's a bad one. He sits down on the ground, arms wrapped around himself. He shivers again. After a moment, as if falling asleep, he simply falls to his side. Unfortunately, he's now in the path of the others. PREACH stops dead in his tracks when he reaches NEEDYDUDE. The others crash into him.

CAL/DOE: Hey, what's going on! Who stopped the line? What're you doing? I've got to be somewhere!

PREACH: I think he's dead.

CAL/DOE: Who? What? What're you talkin' about?

> *All three stand around NEEDYDUDE.*

PREACH: I didn't see him. He was just there. I walked right into him.

CAL: Too bad.

DOE: The poor man. He looks awful. Like he hasn't eaten for days.

PREACH: It's freezing out here. I wished I'd seen him before.

CAL: Aw, there's a rescue mission across town. Besides, Burger King's hiring, right? Come on, I've got to get downtown.

> *The drumbeat suddenly stops. All three look around.*

CAL/DOE/PREACH: Who's there? (They look up.) YOU!? (They point at NEEDYDUDE.) Him? WHAT? WELL, HE SHOULD HAVE ASKED US FOR HELP!

PREACH: I've got a jacket—

DOE (shaking can): I've got something in here—

CAL: Does he take...MasterCard?

> *Silence. They look at NEEDYDUDE, then they look up.*

PREACH/DOE/CAL: That's not fair, Lord...WHY DIDN'T YOU TELL US IT WAS YOU!?

> *BLACKOUT (freeze, then exit)*

73

The Right Equipment

Lawrence G. and Andrea J. Enscoe

Main Theme: Using God's gifts to serve Him.
You may want to use this skit as part of a study of Matthew 25:14-30 or Romans 12:6-8.

Characters
BARRY: A teenager
HOMELESS LADY
GREASE MONKEY: A mechanic
CHAIN MAN: An escaped convict from a chain gang

Props: A large, shiny toolbox, a can of tuna, a coin, oily overalls, handcuffs and leg irons, a garbage can, newspapers.

BARRY runs onstage carrying a large, shiny toolbox.

BARRY (calling off): Dad! Wai—*Dad!* Hold up, will ya! You spaced your tool...I said you *forgot your toolbox!* (He tries to catch his breath.) No, *you* forgot it. (He stops.) What d'you mean? Wait. Time out. What do I want with this thing? No, no, Dad it's your toolbox. Awww, is this one of those "You're a man now, you need your own toolbox" routines? Okay, so it's mine now. Fine. So how long you gonna be gone? Dad? *Dad!* (No reply. He looks at the tool box.) Man, this is great. He couldn't pull the old "You're a man now, you need your own Jaguar" routine. (He unlatches the toolbox.) What am I doing? No way. I touch it and something's gonna break. Guaranteed. (Locks it down.) Yeah, if something happens to anything before he gets back, I'll just tell him I didn't touch a pickin' thing. That's my story.

HOMELESS LADY enters from the opposite side of the stage. BARRY picks up the toolbox and moves off. He passes by the HOMELESS LADY and tries to ignore her.

HOMELESS LADY: Hey. Hey, bub. Hey, palsy.

BARRY: Got no change. (Keeps walking.)

HOMELESS LADY: Shoot. Wait, wait. (She digs in her pocket and pulls out a can of tuna.) Ya gotta can open-er on ya?

BARRY (rolls his eyes; sarcastically): Sure. In my back pocket.

HOMELESS LADY: Where'd you get the toolbox?

BARRY: My father. What do you care—?

HOMELESS LADY: Whadd'ya got in it?

BARRY: I don't know.

HOMELESS LADY: Ain't ya looked in it even?

BARRY: What's it to ya, lady! (Digs in pocket.) Look, I think I do have a quarter here.

HOMELESS LADY: Maybe there's a can opener in there. Ya never know, huh? Why'n'cha open'er up?

BARRY: Trust me. There's no can opener in here!

HOMELESS LADY: Maybe I could use a screwdriver and a hammer or somethin', huh?

74

BARRY (shoving a coin at her): Here's a quarter. I'm not opening the toolbox, okay!

HOMELESS LADY (walks away, mumbling): Why you carry the thing around if ya ain't gonna use it? Sheesh!

GREASE MONKEY (offstage): Hey pal! Hey buddy!

>   *BARRY turns around. He sees the GREASE MONKEY enter in oily overalls and a cap.*

GREASE MONKEY: Hey, you think you gotta trimensional dual-sided spanner in that kit there?

BARRY: Sorry, Scotty. You can't save the Enterprise this time.

GREASE MONKEY: Hey, no really, ya mind I take a look? It'd really help me out. (He goes to BARRY, who backs away, hugging the toolbox.)

BARRY: Get out. You're not looking in my toolbox.

GREASE MONKEY: Come on. That's a spiffy kit there. I'm broke down, huh? One look. Okay?

BARRY: Look! I'm not opening the toolbox! My dad gave it to me. It's his, got it? I'm not gonna use nothin'.

GREASE MONKEY: If your dad gave it to ya, then I'm sure he wouldn't mind—

BARRY: *He minds!*

GREASE MONKEY (throws his hands up in surrender): Okay, okay. Don't get all squirrelly.

>   *GREASE MONKEY goes out. The CHAIN MAN comes in behind BARRY. BARRY sighs and turns around. He yells in surprise at seeing the CHAIN MAN and almost drops the toolbox. The CHAIN MAN has handcuffs and leg irons on.*

CHAIN MAN: Nice toolbox, buddy. You think you got a—

BARRY: *No!*

CHAIN MAN: Maybe a hacksaw or some—

BARRY: *Nothing!*

CHAIN MAN (gestures at the box): What's that there, then?

BARRY (backing away): A mistake, that's what it is. Somebody just gave it to me. I didn't know I was gonna have to do something with it.

CHAIN MAN: Well, hey, can I have it then—?

BARRY: *No! It's mine!* Now start walking. (CHAIN MAN doesn't move.) Officer! *Officer!*

>   *CHAIN MAN looks around, hunted. He hustles out.*

BARRY: Unbelievable. (Looks at the box.) I don't need this grief. None've it! (He looks around. Sees a garbage can a little ways on. He goes and stuffs the toolbox in and covers it up with newspapers.) That'll work. When he comes back, I'll go get the stupid toolbox for him. He ought'a be grateful, anyways. It'll all be in one piece when he gets it. (Pause. Wipes his hands.) Yeah, he should be real happy I took nooo chances with it.

>   *BARRY taps the garbage can twice and goes out, hands stuffed in his pockets.*

>   *BLACKOUT (exit)*

75

Never Too Early to Serve Him

Jim and Lisa Suth

Main Theme: Sharing Jesus with others.
You may want to use this skit as part of a study of Matthew 28:18-20; Romans 1:16 or 10:13,14.

Character
WENDY STYLES

Optional prop: A crumpled sheet of paper.

> *It is suggested that this monologue be played before a group that is very familiar with the skit player, to avoid anyone thinking the skit player is really ill. Have the character who plays WENDY dress differently than usual. Due to the skit's length, it can be read from a crumpled sheet of paper as if it is a personal testimony. It can be performed by a male or female, with minor script changes. You may want to introduce the skit as a dramatization.*

WENDY: Hi! My name is Wendy Styles. I'm 17 years old. I'm like most of you except I'll be dead in four months. Brain cancer. Doctor Walsh said 94 percent never make it to six months. (Small pause.) Don't be surprised that I'm so comfortable with it. I've known for three weeks.

The good news is that I'm a Christian. You wouldn't have been able to tell that three weeks ago. Nothing like finding out you're going to die to fire up your prayer life.

I regret a million things. I guess it's still hard for me to believe that someone who's 17 can die. Especially me. Always thought I'd have that 50th birthday party with all my old friends. I'm not discounting a miracle of course, but I guess I'm ready if God has chosen this as my time. It took a lot of tears to get to that point. (Sigh, almost of relief.)

Some of my friends at school will know that I died, but many of them won't know that I wasn't scared. That's because I blew it. I never shared Christ's promise of salvation with them. I always figured I had so much time. Witnessing was for adults. I always thought my friends would die laughing if I brought up Christ.

That's why I wanted to do talk to you today. I know I've missed a lot of chances. I didn't want to miss this one. If you love Jesus...tell somebody. If you know Jesus...tell somebody. We had a foreign exchange student stay at our house for six months. She went to church with us every Sunday. I never said a word. She's back in France probably telling her friends about our weekly custom. That's because I never told her why we went! She listened to every word I said for six months and I never said, "Jesus loves you." (Her face reflects her regret.) I've waited too long to tell you all this and for that I'm sorry

I can see some of you out there that I've been going to church with since I was five. (She has to stop for a second.) We all did that flannelboard thing, told the stories, memorized the verses. But how many of you guys have told somebody at school that you believe God is real?

If you're in junior high or high school right now, listen to me. You really could be dead tomorrow. There's no cancer history in my family. No heart disease. No nothing. I had an ear infection when I was five, and three stitches in my knee when I was 14. That's it. Then whammo, massive brain tumor. No warning, just a few headaches. My mom and I thought I was allergic to a new perfume or something.

If you're young and I'm scaring you...good. If you're contemplating your life...even better. I want to dare you to live for Christ. Live like you only have three months to live. It's never too early to serve Him. Thank you.

EXIT

The Great SAT of Life
Lawrence G. and Andrea J. Enscoe

Main Theme: Trusting in God.
You may want to use this skit as part of a study of Psalms 62:8; Proverbs 3:5,6; John 14:1 or 2 Corinthians 1:8-11.

Characters
VOICE
CHRIS
MS. NEW-AGE
TIMID TINA
MR. CHECKOUT
CHEATER

Props: Five chairs, five pencils, test-like booklets, a cellular phone, a crystal, a mirror. **Optional**: A chalkboard.

Five anxious students are sitting in chairs—TIMID TINA, MS. NEW-AGE, CHEATER, MR. CHECKOUT and CHRIS. A chalkboard behind reads "The SAT of Life," and "No Talking." The students are all talking.

VOICE (from offstage): Good morning. Welcome, students, to the Great SAT of Life. There will be no talking, eating, chewing gum or drinking during the test. Please fill in each correct bubble on your answer sheet with a Number 2 pencil. Fill in the bubbles completely. Don't take too long on each question. Remember, you have 60 to 70 years to complete the test. You may turn your books over now.

They turn over the books. A collective groan.

ALL: I should'a studied more!

VOICE (offstage): Shhh!

They begin to read. CHEATER rolls back his pant leg and reads notes written on his ankle. MS. NEW-AGE looks around the room. CHRIS, who sits a little bit apart, watches everyone.

CHRIS (to MS. NEW-AGE): Why aren't you working on the test?

MS. NEW-AGE: What test? There is no test. I'm in an out-of-body experience right now. My crystal is warm. There is no test.

CHRIS: Right in front've you. On the table.

MS. NEW-AGE (almost chanting): There is no test....There is no test. (CHRIS holds it up in front of her face.) Oh, that test. (Disgruntled, she begins to read.)

CHEATER has slid off his belt and is reading notes written on the back side of it. TIMID TINA looks around and pulls out a cellular phone from under her jacket.

TIMID TINA (whispering): Mom, I don't have any answers. Help me, will ya? I can't do it alone.

MR. CHECKOUT sits with arms folded, looking ahead.

MS. NEW-AGE (to MR. CHECKOUT): Are you looking for your center?

MR. CHECKOUT: Naw, I'm just not takin' the stupid test.

MS. NEW-AGE: If you can only find your chakras, you'll be able to—

MR. CHECKOUT: Chakra! Get out, Crystal Breath. I'm not takin' the test because nobody's got any answers.

It's a waste'a time. Even if ya came up with an answer and filled in the bubble, it's only your opinion. Got some smoke on ya?

> *MS. NEW-AGE shakes her head, wide-eyed. CHEATER lifts up the collar of the person in front of him and looks for notes.*

TIMID TINA (dials): Hello, Ms. Landers. This is Tina from your history class. I'm not ready for this test. Can you give me some answers? Could you take the test for me?

> *MS. NEW-AGE looks at CHRIS, whose eyes are closed in prayer.*

MS. NEW-AGE (almost squealing): Oh, finding your center!

CHRIS: No. My place.

MS. NEW-AGE: Your place is in the center. The center of everything. You are everything. Want my crystal?

CHRIS: I'm not meditating. I'm praying.

> *Everyone looks at CHRIS.*

MR. CHECKOUT: To God? Dude, give it up. You won't get any answers. One-sided conversation.

MS. NEW-AGE: Well, that's almost like meditating.

CHEATER: Does God have Cliff Notes?

TIMID TINA: You got His phone number?

VOICE (offstage): *Shhhhhh!*

> *They go back to work. MS. NEW-AGE holds a crystal to her forehead. CHRIS goes back to prayer. TIMID TINA dials.*

TIMID TINA: Hello, can you put me through to Mr. Wizard?

> *CHEATER holds up a mirror in an attempt to see the test in front of him.*

CHRIS: Lord, I don't know all the answers. I really don't. I read up all I could. I went to studies and all. It's just, some of these questions I don't know. I don't understand them.

TIMID TINA: Can you put me through to the Mahareeshi Yogibeary?

> *CHEATER pulls a piece of paper out of his nose (or mouth) and reads it. Behind him, MR. CHECKOUT sneezes.*

MS. NEW-AGE (out of her trance): The elements bless you.

MR. CHECKOUT: Get a life, Shirley Maclaine

MS. NEW-AGE: How about two?

CHRIS: Lord, you know my heart. I want to do the right thing. None've these people around here are getting anywhere on this test. They don't have any answers. Mr. Checkout over there doesn't even believe there are any answers. Cheater can't find any answers for himself. (Pointing his thumb at TIMID TINA.) She's callin' everyone in town hoping someone'll take the test for her. New-Age queen here— she doesn't even know she's on the planet. (Sighs.) Well, I'm just gonna start. I'm just gonna pick up this pencil and lean on you.

MS. NEW-AGE: There is no test. No test. I float on clouds of warm liquid. No test...no test..

MR. CHECKOUT: No answers. There are no answers. I'd kill for some Jack Daniels.

TIMID TINA: Whad'ya mean Mother Theresa won't take a collect call?

> *CHEATER takes off his shoe and reads notes on his foot.*

CHRIS: Thank you for my brains, my common sense and your direction. I commit myself to you. (He picks up his pencil and starts working.)

> *BLACKOUT (freeze, then exit)*

78

Baal Me Out

Jim and Lisa Suth

Main Theme: God is all-powerful.

You may want to use this skit as part of a study of 1 Kings 18:16-39; 1 Chronicles 29:10-13; Isaiah 40:22-31 or Ephesians 1:18-21.

This is a group participation skit based on 1 Kings 18:16-39. Choose individuals to represent Elijah, Ahab, Jezebel and the Bull, then divide the remaining parts among the remaining participants. Tell the participants what their lines are. When each character's name is read, he or she says the given line.

Characters and Lines
ELIJAH: "Lord, show Your power."
AHAB: "Oh yeah? So what?"
PROPHETS OF BAAL: "Bail us out, Baal."
PROPHETS OF ASHERAH: "Watch us dance and shout."
PEOPLE: "Oooh—ahhh."
WATERBEARERS: "This stuff is heavy!"
JEZEBEL: "Boy, do I love idols!"
BULL: "Moooooo."

NARRATOR (reading slowly to allow for character lines): Once there was a prophet of God by the name of **Elijah**. He was not on the best of terms with **King Ahab** of Israel or his wife **Jezebel**. In fact, **Elijah** was in hiding to save his life.

However, the time came for **Elijah** to confront **Ahab** about his sin of idol worship. **King Ahab** had abandoned God's commands and was following the teachings of Baal. So **Elijah** met with **Ahab** and proposed the following plan to proclaim to **Ahab, Jezebel**, and the **people** that God is powerful and mighty.

Elijah called for the **people** to meet him on Mount Carmel. There he challenged the **prophets of Baal** and the **prophets of Asherah** to a duel. The **prophets of Baal** and the **prophets of Asherah** would prepare a **bull** for sacrifice, but not light the fire on the altar; **Elijah** would also prepare a **bull** but not light the fire. Then each would call upon their god and whichever one answered by sending down fire would be proclaimed the most powerful. **Elijah** even let the **prophets of Baal** and the **prophets of Asherah** go first.

From morning until noon, the **prophets of Baal** and the **prophets of Asherah** called out to their god but received no answer, and the **people** watched and waited. At mid-day, **Elijah** began to kid the prophets saying their god was busy traveling or perhaps sleeping. The **prophets of Baal** and the **prophets of Asherah** shouted louder and danced faster. As the **people** watched, the prophets began to cut themselves with knives and spears. Still no answer.

Finally evening came and **Elijah** stepped forward. He called the **people** to help repair the altar of God which **Ahab** and **Jezebel** had destroyed. Then **Elijah** dug a trench around the altar and prepared his **bull** for sacrifice. He called for the **waterbearers** to pour water over the offering, and they covered the **bull** and the wood completely. A second time, **Elijah** called the **waterbearers** to pour water on the sacrifice, and finally, a third time **Elijah** had the **waterbearers** soak the **bull** and the wood. Now the offering was drenched and the trench around the altar was full of water. **Elijah** prayed to God, asking for an answer by fire so that the **people** would turn their hearts back to God.

In a flash, the **bull,** the wood, the stones, the soil and all the water that the **waterbearers** had brought were consumed by the fire of the Lord. The **people** were amazed and said, "The Lord—He is God."

Through **Elijah's** faith he had shown that God—our God—is a powerful God.

OPTIONAL LEADER'S TAG: Sometimes it seems like nothing ever goes right. Life is too tough and we don't have the ability to make things work out. And sometimes God seems far away. Soon after Elijah witnessed God torching the dripping wet sacrifice, Elijah got discouraged. It seems kind of ridiculous, when you think about it. God had proved Himself to be not only all-powerful, but always faithful. And He is that for us, too. He will be there for us when we need Him, and He will give us the strength to make it through hard times. Sometimes we forget how powerful our God is. But our Father in heaven is Lord of the universe. He is all we need.

The Invisible Friend

Judith L. Roth

Main Theme: God is sufficient.
You may want to use this skit as part of a study of Psalms 32:7; 62:1,2; 73:23-26; Matthew 11:28-30 or John 16:33.

Characters
BILL: A middle-aged business man
JESSE: A homeless child, seven to nine years old

Props: A bench, a newspaper, a sack lunch, a sandwich.

> *BILL is sitting on a park bench, reading a newspaper and eating his lunch. JESSE walks up and stares at him until BILL looks up.*

BILL: You want something?

JESSE: Mister, I have a friend.

BILL: Oh. That's nice.

> *BILL goes back to his paper and his lunch. JESSE continues to stare at BILL. After a moment, BILL looks up again.*

JESSE: Mister, I said I have a friend.

BILL: I know. I said that was nice.

JESSE: But He's right here. You want to meet Him?

> *BILL looks all around, sees nothing. He looks back at JESSE. His expression registers understanding.*

BILL: Oh, I get it. It's one of those invisible friends. (He puts out his hand to shake the hand of the invisible friend.) Pleased to meet you.

JESSE (amused): He's not *there*.

BILL (tiring of the game): Okay. Just trying to be friendly. Uh, doesn't your mother want you or something?

JESSE: She's at the grocery store.

BILL: That's good. (He continues with his lunch and paper.)

JESSE: Mister, sometimes when I'm lonely, my friend hugs me real tight. Do you want Him to hug you, too?

BILL: Thanks. I'm not lonely.

JESSE: Never?

BILL: What is this? Twenty questions?

JESSE: Do you got a Daddy?

BILL: Not anymore. Do you?

JESSE: He had to go away. That's why Mommy goes to the grocery store.

BILL (with a puzzled expression): That makes sense.

JESSE: Yeah. But my friend takes care of me.

BILL: Does your, um, mommy work at the store?

JESSE: She just goes to get the food they throw out. Sometimes it's yucky. You ever eat raw brussel sprouts? But once there was a whole bunch of cheese that was only kinda moldy.

> *BILL looks down at his lunch. He seems to have lost his appetite.*

BILL: Would you, ah, care for a sandwich?

JESSE: Are you kidding?! Thanks! (He reaches out for the sandwich, looks up at his invisible friend). Thanks!

BILL (looking up, too): Oh, that's where your friend is?

JESSE: Sort of. Like I said, He takes care of me. He brought me over here and look what I got! (Holds up the sandwich.)

BILL (smiling sadly): Yeah.

> *JESSE goes and sits beside the man on the bench.*

Where do you live?

JESSE: Well, we sort of don't got a place right now. Hey, if you ever do get lonely, I could share my friend with you.

BILL: Is that why you talk about your friend all the time? Because you don't have a home?

JESSE (confused): I don't think so. If you got a friend, you talk about 'em. Don't you got any friends?

BILL (somewhat defensively): Well, sure I do.

JESSE: Then how come you're sitting here all alone? Hey, do you got an invisible friend, too?

> *BILL starts to say something, then shakes his head. He looks up and sees something in the distance.*

BILL: Do you know that lady? She's waving at you.

JESSE (looking): That's my mommy. I gotta go.

> *JESSE gets up and waves in the direction of his mother. He turns to the man.*

Do you want my friend to stay with you? He could keep you company.

BILL: Thanks, but I don't really need an invisible friend right now.

JESSE: Really? That's funny, cuz my friend Jesus is *all* that I need. Well, see ya, Mister!

> *JESSE runs off towards his mother. BILL watches him go. BILL looks up heavenward and then thoughtfully gazes after JESSE.*
>
> *BLACKOUT (freeze, then exit)*

The Emmaus Tunnel

Jim & Lisa Suth

Main Theme: God is all-powerful.
You may want to use this skit as part of a study of Isaiah 40:22-31; Ephesians 1:18-21 or 2 Peter 1:3.

Characters
JOHN: The driver
SANDRA: John's girlfriend
MARTIN: John's friend
BILL: A hitchhiker

Props: Four chairs, two flashlights, schoolbooks, a shirt and tie, a small Bible.

> *John and Sandra are waiting in John's car in the school parking lot to give Martin a ride. They have flashlights hidden for use later on in the skit.*

JOHN: I hope he didn't get detention or something stupid like that. Does he know we're waiting out here?

SANDRA: Yes, for the third time. Will you please chill. (Looks in rear view mirror.) You're gonna give me crows feet on my eyes from your stress. I saw him at break. Quit freaking out, he'll be here.

JOHN: Sorry. I'm starving. (Knightly.) I am on a quest, milady, to secure massive amounts of quality fast-food grub in order to obtain your favor.

SANDRA: You are not from this planet, you—oh, there he is.

JOHN: Finally. My blood sugar was getting low. Oh no! He has that look.

SANDRA: What look?

JOHN: It's hard to describe. Kind of....

MARTIN (dropping books to rap): How do my friends, you're looking mighty cool, your main man Martin is now out of school. Let's fly this jalopy to some food we be jammin', I'll grab some grub down my throat I'll be slammin'. And if you think that my rap lacks drive, I'm your main man Martin, I don't take no jive!

> *JOHN laughs, completely losing control. SANDRA looks mortified.*

SANDRA (yelling out the window): I don't know either of these people! I am being held against my will!

JOHN (wiping tears of laughter from his eyes; to MARTIN): Main man, can I have your autograph?

MARTIN: John. I'm in love.

JOHN and SANDRA (looking at each other): Again.

MARTIN: No really. I think she likes me.

JOHN and SANDRA: Again.

MARTIN (undaunted): Hey, get this question I heard in science today: Can God make a rock so big He can't lift it?

JOHN: Of course, He made your brain so small you can't find it! Would you get in the car already? I'm at death's door for lack of greasy food.

> *MARTIN hops in the two-door car, crawling over JOHN's back to get to the back seat. JOHN pulls out into traffic and begins the drive.*

SANDRA: McDee's?

JOHN: Taco Bell. There's a burrito waiting for me.

MARTIN: Pizza. A combo represents all four food groups.

JOHN: I'm driving.

SANDRA and MARTIN: Taco Bell sounds great.

JOHN: Stop and go, I can't believe it. I hate this parkway.

MARTIN: It's too early. There must have been an accident.

> *They sit in silence for a while, rolling forward a car length at a time.*

SANDRA: Now I'm hungry.

JOHN: Look at this guy hitching. He must have run out of gas.

MARTIN: Nice tie, too. That'll be a goner soon.

JOHN: Let's give him a ride.

> *Both MARTIN and SANDRA look at JOHN shocked.*

SANDRA: I thought you were hungry. Now we have time for this guy?

MARTIN (uneasy): I don't think that's such a great idea, John. What if he tries to pound on us or something?

JOHN: Give me a break, Martin. What are the chances of that happening? He's wearing a tie. Besides, there's three of us.

SANDRA: Two of you. I'm not helping you beat up anybody.

JOHN (ignoring the fighting aspect): We're not going anywhere fast. Give the guy a break. It's freezing out there.

MARTIN: Okay, okay, Cut through this parking lot and we can take the tunnel. If he's going that way, cool. If not, sorry.

JOHN: Deal.

> *JOHN pulls over and up to hitchhiker. BILL enters and comes to SANDRA's side. JOHN rolls down SANDRA's window and leans over to speak.*

Where you headed?

BILL: My car stalled on the other side of the tunnel. Just get me back through the tunnel and I'll be fine.

JOHN (to MARTIN and SANDRA): See?! Hop in, uh....

BILL: Bill. Thanks a million for stopping. I thought I was gonna have to hoof it the whole way.

> *SANDRA gets out so BILL can climb in the back seat. Then SANDRA climbs back in. JOHN pulls back into traffic.*

JOHN: You might get there faster by walking, Bill. This traffic is brutal.

BILL: That's okay. At least I'm out of the cold.

MARTIN: Uh...Bill. I'm Martin. (They shake hands.) Nice to meet you. (BILL nods.) Would you mind if I asked you a question?

BILL: Fire away.

MARTIN: We've never met so you can be very honest about your answer. Can God make a rock so big He can't lift—

84

JOHN: You dork! He just wants a ride. He doesn't care about—

BILL: God is all-powerful. He can do anything He wants. He is God.

The car is silent. BILL's response has surprised everyone.

SANDRA: You sound like my Dad!

JOHN: If God was all-powerful, He'd get us out of this traffic jam.

MARTIN: Man, God doesn't care about that stuff. Earthquakes, tornadoes, floods. That's His department.

BILL: Martin, Luke 12:7 says: "The very hairs of your head are numbered." Matthew 6:26 says that God even makes sure that the birds have something to eat. God knows what color socks you put on this morning. He cares about things that small.

SANDRA: Hey, traffic cleared up.

Everyone turns to look at BILL. He shrugs knowingly.

JOHN: You don't think He did that, do you?

BILL: What do you think?

JOHN: I don't think so. What about you? He let your car run out of gas.

BILL: You're giving me a ride, aren't you? (Silence.) Jesus said in Matthew 17:20 that if you have faith as small as a mustard seed, you can tell a mountain to move and it will.

MARTIN: Sounds like you've known God a long time, though. I can't have that much faith. I need more proof.

BILL: Here, I have this little Bible. (He pulls a small Bible from his pocket.) I'd like you to read this passage right here.

He hands the Bible over to MARTIN. As soon as MARTIN gets the Bible there is an immediate blackout. As soon as darkness is complete, BILL should exit as quickly and as quietly as possible. JOHN and SANDRA both pull their hidden flashlights out and turn them on to represent headlights.

JOHN: All right, the tunnel! Look for cracks everybody!

SANDRA (slapping JOHN's shoulder in the dark): Don't do that. You know I hate it. You think it's funny—I don't.

MARTIN (as if it's a big joke): I'd love to read this passage, Bill, but it's a little dark in here. Hey. I think,...Bill,...Bill,.... *You guys, Bill's not in the car anymore!!*

JOHN: Maybe he saw his car and got out.

MARTIN: We're going thirty and this is a two-door! Did he crawl over either of your backs to get out?!!

SANDRA: I don't like this at all, guys. This isn't funny.

Full lights. Actors douse flashlights.

JOHN: Holy smokes, you're not kidding. He's gone!

MARTIN: Listen to this passage you guys. Luke 24:31-32. "Then their eyes were opened and they recognized him, and he disappeared from their sight. They asked each other, 'Were not our hearts burning within us while he talked with us on the road and opened the Scriptures to us?'"

There is silence in the car for a moment.

SANDRA: Maybe God *can* do whatever He wants.

BLACKOUT (freeze, then exit)

This Race Is Your Life
Jim and Lisa Suth

Main Theme: Persevering in faith.
You may want to use this skit as part of a study of 1 Corinthians 9:25; Philippians 3:12-14; Colossians 1:10-12; Hebrews 12:1-3 or James 1:4.

BOB: Sports newscaster
BETTY: Sports newscaster
BIFF: Roving reporter
BILL: Roving reporter
BRETT: Roving reporter
TEMPTATION CHEERLEADER #1
TEMPTATION CHEERLEADER #2
TEMPTATION CHEERLEADER #3

Props: Two chairs, a chart showing the track, three cheerleader costumes including pom-poms, a can of Pepsi, a bag of Cheetos, a box of Desitin.

BOB and BETTY are in a sportscaster's booth on stage. BIFF, BILL and BRETT are planted in the audience—BIFF in the fourth row, BILL near the back and BRETT near the front right corner of the audience.

BOB: Hello, and welcome to the perennial running of "The Race of Your Life." I'm Bob Boone along with Betty Brown here to help you look in on the action of day to day "running the race." Betty?

BETTY: That's right, Bob. For some of the competitors it's been a long road to this point just to get in shape to compete. Bob, let's look at the track.

BOB holds up a chart with a cross on the bottom left and a crown on the top right. The track is a straight line.

BOB: Right, Betty. As you can see from this aerial view, the race starts here at the beginning of your life with Christ, and finishes here with your reward in heaven. Let's go to Biff live at the starting line.

BIFF (popping up suddenly and speaking loudly as if outside): We're here at the starting line and there certainly is a lot of excitement! The path is wide and all are newcomers to this competition. Oh...wait a minute...there's the gun. All of the runners have accepted Christ and they're off! (Looking over audience as if seeing the action) There seems to be quite a bit of jockeying for position here in the beginning stages of the race. We'll keep an eye out for major leader changes. Back to Bob and Betty in the booth.

BETTY: Thank you, Biff. Well, as the race is progressing, let's go to some other sports news. Bob?

BOB: Undefeated and untied Goliath of Gath—looking for his forty-seventh straight victory—was upset by young upstart David of Israel. Final score, Israel 1, Philistines 0. David was asked how he was able to pull off such a major upset and he was quoted as saying, "I had faith in my God. He will never fail me." Great comeback for little David of Israel. Betty?

BETTY: The seventh lap around Jericho was disrupted by a large earthquake today. Sources say the race will not be completed due to the extensive damage to Jericho. We'll have more news in a minute, after this word.

The TEMPTATION CHEERLEADERS jump out on center stage. They line up with respective products in hand.

CHEERLEADER #1: Try Pepsi, it's the very best!

CHEERLEADER #2: Try Bud, it's better than the rest!

CHEERLEADER #3: Desitin, if you want to win!

CHEERLEADERS #1,2,3: Try them all, they're better than sin! Try something. Try anything. Just as long as you try it. It'll be great! YEAH! (They send their pom-poms flying.)

BOB: The cheerleaders have made very tempting offers, Betty. That could discourage our runners from competing to the best of their abilities.

BETTY: It certainly could, Bob. All of those things are (pause) temporal. Let's go to Bill for a race update. Bill?

BILL (popping up near the back): Thanks, Betty. We're here at about a third of the way through the race. It's been very interesting to see who chose the correct path at this juncture. The 50-foot-wide easy freeway path you see to your right is not part of the original course. This small narrow path to your left over the rocks and broken glass is the actual course route. Each participant was given this map at the beginning of the race (holds up Bible). Some runners still seem to get off track at this fork in the road and only half of our original contestants are still heading for the goal line. Back to Bob.

BIFF: Me?

BILL: No, *Bob!*

BIFF: Sorry!

BOB: While we're waiting for race updates, let's go to the news. Betty?

BETTY: Thanks, Bill. Sorry, I mean Bob. The apostle Paul is in the news again today. His Roman citizenship made him eligible to receive the Caesars Gold Leaf Award for amazing endurance. Paul survived another riot and a full fledged stoning. As usual, Paul was quoted as saying, "For to me to live is Christ and to die is gain." Paul's uncommon faith may make him eligible for sportsman of the year. His—

BOB: Sorry, Betty. Late breaking race news. Let's go to Brett.

BIFF and BILL (standing): Who?

BOB: Brett!

BIFF and BILL (sitting again): Oh.

BRETT (jumps up; jogging in place as if keeping up with the runners): We're almost at the end of the race, Bob. This has been amazing to watch. Some of the runners have fallen a number of times, but they keep getting up and running. This has been the ultimate in endurance. The winner of today's race will be the one who perseveres to the fullest.

BETTY: What's happening out there, Brett? Tell us about the race.

BRETT: Well, Betty, as the runners press on toward the goal they will face some of their worst temptations yet. We're nearing the bandstand now and I can hear the Temptation Cheerleaders goading on the runners.

CHEERLEADERS (jumping to center stage; cheering in sing song): You ain't gonna make it, hey, hey! You're never gonna make it, no way! You ain't gonna make it, hey, hey! You're never gonna make it, no way!

CHEERLEADERS continue chanting quietly during BRETT's next lines.

BRETT (still jogging): This is incredible! Bob, Betty, Biff and Bill, you should see this! Thirty people tripped near the bandstand and those who were running ahead actually came back to help them up. There's massive confusion near the finish line now as runners check each other for broken bones and dust off contestants who have fallen. Some are limping, some staggering. Wait! They seem to have remembered where they are headed. They're running to the finish line....You should *see* this. Some runners are carrying disabled runners, others have their arms around limping runners and are helping them to the line. It's amazing. A huge crowd at the finish. The winners! They've made it! What incredible perseverance and stamina!

BOB: What a Cinderella story, Betty. What an incredible turn of events in this race. I guess there's never just one winner. Everyone has a chance to make it. Well, I'm Bob Boone....

BETTY: And I'm Betty Brown saying, So long from The Race of Your Life. And remember, you can make it, too!

BLACKOUT (freeze, then exit)

A Costly Pair of Shoes

Barbara D. Larsen

Main Theme: Following wise advice.
You may want to use this skit as part of a study of Proverbs 12:15 or 19:20.

Characters
KEVIN: Teenage track runner
STEVE: A fellow runner
COACH: School track coach

Props: Two long benches, two track uniforms, a sweat suit, tennis shoes, a Walkman cassette player, shorts, a T-shirt, a whistle.

> *The scene is a school locker room containing two long benches. STEVE, wearing a track uniform, enters listening to a Walkman radio. He "jives" to silent music as he walks to a bench and is seated. He snaps his fingers, taps his feet and sways in time to the music. He begins to take off his shoes as KEVIN enters, also wearing a track uniform, limping and groaning in evident pain. KEVIN drags himself to the other bench and drops heavily onto it.*

KEVIN: Yowee!! Am I glad this practice is over! My feet are killing me. Those last two laps were so painful I didn't think I was gonna make it! It was awful! (Holds up each foot in turn and looks it over) Ohhh! They hurt like everything!

STEVE (noticing; lifts up one earphone): Feet give out on you again? Sorry, Kevin. Seems like you keep having this problem! They really are sore, huh?

KEVIN: You don't know the half of it, Steve, old buddy. Man, I didn't think I could drag myself to the locker room! (Gingerly takes off a shoe) Ouch! Ow! I can't stand it!

STEVE: I feel for you, guy. Let me see. (He looks.) Hey, that's terrible, Kev! It's all bloody! Maybe you broke a blister or something.

KEVIN: Yeah...I must have. Boy, what a mess! And all my toes are raw! They feel paralyzed. I can't bear to touch 'em! Ow!

STEVE: Hey, what're you going to do? The All-City Track Meet is tomorrow. You'll never run on feet like that. What'll you tell Coach?

KEVIN: I don't know, I don't know.

> *KEVIN takes off the other shoe as COACH enters and overhears. COACH is wearing shorts and a T-shirt and has a whistle around his neck. He is a military type, commanding respect from the boys.*

Ohh! Ouch! This toot's even worse! It's bleeding and swollen, too! Why'd this have to happen to me? (Long groan.) ·

> *STEVE goes back to listening to the Walkman.*

COACH: What's the trouble, here? (Sees KEVIN's feet.) Oh, no, Kevin, not again! Look at those feet. They are *gross!* Did that just happen today?

KEVIN (reluctantly): Not really, sir. It's been coming on all week. I didn't want to tell you, but every practice it's a little worse.

89

COACH stoops over and picks up KEVIN's shoes. He holds them in the air, one in each hand. STEVE is curious and lifts one earphone.

COACH: And no wonder! Are you still wearing these shoes?

KEVIN: Well...sir...I....

COACH: What size shoe do you wear?

KEVIN: Eleven and a half, sir!

COACH: And what size are these shoes?

KEVIN: Ten, sir!

COACH (aghast): I can't believe it! I told you three weeks ago to get rid of these horrors. You missed the marathon last month because your feet hurt, remember?

KEVIN (uncomfortable with these questions): Uh...yes...sir!

COACH: And we lost one whole event because you went lame on your lap of the relay at last Friday's meet. True?

KEVIN: Uh, I guess so...sir!

> *COACH is exasperated. He tosses the shoes to the floor. He paces as he lectures, kicking a shoe like a football as he passes it. STEVE listens to COACH as he puts on his sweatsuit, keeping the earphones to one ear.*

COACH: Kevin, what *is* it with you? I explained to you how...how *foolish* it was to keep on wearing these...these...monstrosities!...because they were giving you blisters and...and cramping your toes, and making it impossible for you to hit your stride. Didn't we talk about this and decide that the shoes were *wrong* for you?

KEVIN: Yeah...we sorta did...sir!

> *STEVE moves closer and listens more intently, earphones now pushed back.*

COACH (flabbergasted): Well, why...*why*, in the name of sanity, tell me, why are you still wearing the stupid things and suffering such torment?

KEVIN (explaining feebly): Aw, Coach. I love these shoes, and, and, they cost eighty dollars, and look, they have our school colors on the sides, and...(running out of steam) and everything. Sir.

COACH: You aren't making any sense, Kevin. You're talking foolishness. You know I told you to throw the things out, but you persist in this dumb, block-headed, absurd—oh, I give up! You're going to sacrifice your whole career in track. I'll end up having to drop you from the team just because you won't listen to reason—you won't listen to wisdom.

> *KEVIN retrieves the shoes from where COACH has thrown them. He is still stubborn. He begins to put the shoes on again, very carefully.*

KEVIN: Maybe the shoes *are* ruining my life, but hey, it's *my* life. So I have to make up my own mind. Even if you're right, it doesn't mean I have to do what you're saying. (Pause.) Sir!

STEVE: Hey, Kev, c'mon! Use your head! Coach is only trying to help you solve your problem. If you'd just pay attention....

KEVIN (slowly standing, grimacing at feet): I can't, Steve. You don't understand.

STEVE: But he's right! Get rid of those shoes. It's the only sensible thing for you to do! Coach is right!

KEVIN (annoyed): I don't care if he's right! I need to find my *own* solution, not anyone else's. I'll come up with something one of these days. So maybe I'll throw 'em out and maybe I won't...but I'll decide for myself what to do! (Groaning, he limps out.) Talk to you guys later.

COACH shakes his head sadly as he and STEVE watch KEVIN leave.

STEVE: What a loon! What's the matter with him, anyway? It's like he doesn't even care about the damage he's doing to himself!

COACH: You got it, Steve! You know, there's a proverb in the Bible that says a fool thinks he needs no advice...but a *wise man* listens to others.

COACH turns to STEVE and points his finger.

COACH (shouting): And now, Mister, about that Walkman you've been wearing all week at practice...

STEVE jerks to attention, grabbing at the radio in guilty surprise.

STEVE: Sir??!

BLACKOUT (freeze, then exit)

Free Time
Kathy Pocsics

Main Theme: Discerning healthy thoughts and activities.
You may want to use this skit as part of a study of Ephesians 5:15,16; Philippians 4:8,9 or Colossians 3:16.

Characters
DENNIS: Man recently laid off
SHARON: Dennis's wife
VOICE #1: News commentator
LOIS: Next-door neighbor
VOICE #2: Soap opera actor
VOICE #3: Soap opera actress
JESSICA: Sharon's friend
VOICE #4: Character from a western
VOICE #5: Character from a western
JULIE: Teenager

Props: A couch, a newspaper, a TV Guide, a TV remote control, a paperback book, a Bible study guide, a Bible, a doorbell sound, an exercise outfit, a ticket. **Optional:** A coffee table.

DENNIS sits on a couch. A coffee table holds a newspaper, TV Guide, remote TV control, paper back book and Bible study guide. SHARON enters.

SHARON: Well, how do I look for my first day of work?

DENNIS (disinterested): Fine.

SHARON: Not that a job at Disneyland could be called work! I'm almost glad you got laid off.

DENNIS: Well, at least one of us is happy about it.

SHARON: I didn't mean it like that. You'll find something soon.

DENNIS: I hope so.

SHARON: And in the meantime, I get to go to Disneyland free! And you can spend time studying your Bible like you've always wanted to.

DENNIS: Right.

SHARON: Well, I've got to go. Have fun today. I know I will!

SHARON exits. DENNIS looks at his Bible for a moment. Then he notices the newspaper.

DENNIS: Maybe I ought to read the paper before I get into my Bible study. Got to keep up on world events to be a good Christian!

DENNIS opens the newspaper and reads it as an offstage voice is heard.

VOICE #1: Mr. Jake Livingston of Cedar Grove was shot and killed yesterday in his own home by a next-door neighbor. Mr. Livingston's wife discovered his dead body on the living room floor. The newspaper he was reading at the time was scattered around the room.

A doorbell is heard. DENNIS jumps, dropping his newspaper. He stares at the door, too startled to move. LOIS enters.

LOIS (speaking rapidly): Dennis, are you still here? I guess you haven't found a job yet. I saw Sharon leave a few minutes ago. She's going to love working at Disneyland. Anyway, I was baking a cake and ran out of sugar. Do you have some I could borrow? (Exits, continuing lines offstage. DENNIS watches her, silently.) Oh, dear, you seem to be out of sugar. You'd better run to the supermarket, Dennis, and pick up some more. Looks like you could use flour, too. (Re-enters) Well, I've got to get back home. Can't miss "All My Children," you know! (Exits.)

DENNIS: I can't believe I felt *afraid* of my own next-door neighbor! Lois wouldn't shoot anyone. She wouldn't *have* to—she could *talk* them to death! (He chuckles at his own joke and sits back down.) "All My Children"! Is that what women do all day, watch soap operas? (He glances at the *TV Guide*.) I wonder what channel that's on. I mean, with so many people watching it every day, there must be something to it. Maybe I'll just watch one episode so I'll know what everyone is talking about.

DENNIS checks the TV Guide, then turns on the TV by remote control.

VOICE #2 (softly): What are you doing here?

VOICE #3 (romantically): I came to see *you*, of course.

VOICE #2: You shouldn't have come.

VOICE #3: I had to. I couldn't help myself.

DENNIS: Oh, brother. This is trash!

DENNIS turns off the TV by remote control. The doorbell rings. DENNIS goes to the door. JESSICA enters in an attractive exercise outfit.

DENNIS: Jessica! What are you doing here?

JESSICA: I came to pick up Sharon for aerobics. Is she here?

DENNIS (nervous): No, she's...uh...she's gone right now.

JESSICA: You mean you're here alone?

DENNIS: Well, I...guess so. Is there...anything I can do for you?

JESSICA: No. I'm sorry. I guess I shouldn't have come.

DENNIS (mimicking romantic voice): You had to. You couldn't help yourself.

JESSICA: I beg your pardon?

DENNIS: Oh! Nothing. Never mind. I'll tell Sharon you stopped by.

JESSICA (looking at him strangely): Thanks. (She exits.)

DENNIS: That was strange. No more soaps for me!

DENNIS starts to pick up the Bible again, then sees the paperback book.

DENNIS: That's it! A good western is just what I need to get me in the mood for more serious reading. (He picks up the book and opens it.) Let's see, I was in the middle of chapter four last night. (Reads silently.)

VOICE #4: Get to the point!

VOICE #5: It's about that outlaw you've been tracking, sir.

VOICE #4: That dirty, rotten, low-down...

The doorbell rings.

DENNIS: Honestly! I don't see how housewives get anything done with the doorbell ringing all the time! (He puts down the book and saunters to the door like a bowlegged cowboy. Julie is there.)

DENNIS (roughly): What do you want?

JULIE: I'm sorry, sir. Forgive me for bothering you, but...

DENNIS: Get to the point!

JULIE (quickly): I came to give you a free ticket to our school's car wash. (She hands DENNIS a ticket and exits swiftly.)

DENNIS: I must be going crazy. Maybe I'd better stick to my Bible study, after all. (Opens the Bible study guide.) "Read Philippians 4:8." Okay. (Opens his Bible and finds the passage.) "Finally, brothers, whatever is true, whatever is noble, whatever is right, whatever is pure, whatever is lovely, whatever is admirable—if anything is excellent or praiseworthy—think about such things."

> *DENNIS pauses, contemplating this verse. SHARON enters, flips off her shoes, and collapses on the couch next to DENNIS.*

SHARON: What a day I've had! I thought it would be *fun* to work at Disneyland: dressing up as Snow White, dancing in the parade, serving frozen juice bars! But no, I get stuck with parking lot duty! I stood out in the hot sun all day long directing traffic! (Sigh.) So what did you do today, Honey?

DENNIS: Oh, nothing much. I held a killer at bay while she inventoried our kitchen supplies....I resisted the advances of our sexy neighbor....I scared off a dirty, low-down outlaw who wanted to wash our car. (Pause.) And I learned something about the kinds of things I *should* be letting my mind dwell on.

SHARON (who has been too busy rubbing her feet to hear anything DENNIS has said): That's nice, Dear. (Yawns.) I wonder what's on TV.

DENNIS: Let's not watch TV tonight. I've got a much better idea.

> *DENNIS moves closer to SHARON, puts his arm around her shoulders, and looks into her eyes. SHARON gives him a "Please, Dear, not now" look.*

DENNIS: Let's read a Bible story together!

> *BLACKOUT (freeze, then exit)*

Ham Sandwich

Barbara D. Larsen

Main Theme: Being careful about what you put in your mind.
You may want to use this skit as part of a study of Ephesians 5:4-12 or Philippians 4:8,9.

JASON: A teenager
MOM: Jason's mother

Props: A phone, a counter, a table, two chairs, a trash can, a plate of food covered with garbage including a banana peel, a fork.

JASON is sitting in his room at one side of the stage. MOM is busy working at a kitchen counter on the opposite side. A table and chairs are in the kitchen with a trash can nearby.

JASON (dials phone): Hi, Mrs. Miller, this is Jason. Is Brad there? Thanks. (Pause.) Yo, Brad! How's it going, dude? (Pause.) Aw, not cool, not cool! Yeah. Yeah. Well, I'm sorry, but the deal's off for tonight. (Pause.) I did ask them and they said no. I can't go. (Pause.) Hey, look, it's not my fault. Can I help it if my parents are prehistoric? They don't want me to see that movie. (Pause.) Because it's rated *R* for one thing. (Pause.) I know, I know. I told them everybody's going to it, but they just said, (mocking parent's voice) "Not everybody. You're not!" It might damage my character or something. I shouldn't see all that *baad* stuff. (Pause) Hey, you're not telling me anything I don't already know! Listen, that's exactly what I told my mom. "Mom," I said, "basically it's a great plot, it's a good clean story...that's the main thing. All that language you think is obscene, the violence and sex, that's just the *background*, it's not important. After all," I said, "these are the 90s...things are different now. Not like when you were a kid. The things I see and hear every day at school are as bad as anything I'd see at this movie." (Pause.) Naw, she didn't buy it and neither did my dad. You know what they said? I mean besides not wanting me to go? Get this! They actually told me it was a bad example to others for a Christian to be caught up in worldly things. (Pause.) Yeah, you're right. Sometimes being a Christian is too demanding. It's a bummer, all right!

MOM walks to center stage, toward JASON's room, calling.

MOM: Jason! Lunch is ready! (Returns to kitchen.)

JASON: Yeah, I know what you mean. Hey, dude, I gotta go. Time for the sandwich scene. Well, you guys have a blast tonight, anyway. See ya!

JASON crosses to the table and sits down. MOM places a plate of "food" in front of him, then returns to work at the counter. JASON looks at the plate.

JASON: Hey! What *is* this, anyway? It looks awful!

MOM (turning): It's a ham sandwich, dear.

JASON (disgusted): A ham sandwich! Where? You mean it's buried under here somewhere? (He lifts up a banana peel with his fork.) Look! There's a banana peel on top of it! Yuck! And what's this other junk?

MOM: Oh, that's garbage, Jason. You don't mind a little garbage, do you? After all, it's basically a good clean sandwich. That's all that matters, right? Forget about the rest, that's just the setting the sandwich is in. Go ahead and eat it.

JASON: *Mommm!* I can't eat this junk! It makes me sick just to look at it. Even thinking about it makes me sick!

MOM: Why, you see a lot worse stuff than that every day in the trash can. I'm surprised at you, having such a fit over a little garbage! Can't you just scrape it off and eat it anyway?

JASON (indignant): There's no way I can clean up this sandwich so it's decent to eat!

> *JASON holds up the sandwich, which is dripping and horrible-looking. He drops it back onto the plate.*

I'm not gonna put this gross, rotten stuff in my mouth!

MOM: I'm glad to hear that, Jason. (Pauses for emphasis.) Now I hope you'll be just as careful about what you put into your mind.

> *MOM removes the plate and takes it to the trash can where she dumps it. JASON finally catches on, makes a face and groans.*

Gotcha!

JASON (good-naturedly): Yeah, yeah. You got me. (He rolls his eyes.)

> *BLACKOUT (freeze, then exit)*

The In-Crowd

Barbara D. Larsen

Main Theme: Conforming to Christ, not the world.
You may want to use this skit as part of a study of Romans 12:1,2; Galatians 1:10 or 1 Peter 1:14-16.

Characters
JAN: A teenager
CAROL: Jan's friend
GIRL: A student
THE IN-CROWD: Six to eight teenagers

Props: T-shirts, jeans, suspenders, sneakers, neckties, sunglasses and headbands for eight to ten girls. Textbooks, a bench.

> *The IN-CROWD is dressed alike in T-shirts, jeans, suspenders and sneakers with the other props in their pockets. The CROWD moves together in close formation at all times, walking tightly bunched together in a quick-stepping manner from place to place. They separate just enough to perform each action, returning afterward to close formation, holding their pose until their next move. One person is designated leader for the rest to follow. JAN and CAROL are typical students, dressed appropriately, but not in jeans. Carrying textbooks, they enter talking and sit on a bench at stage left.*

JAN: I can't believe that Mr. Richards! He gave us enough homework to sink the Titanic. And it's due tomorrow. I'll be lucky if I finish half of it by tomorrow.

CAROL: I know what you mean. But I don't see why you're worrying. You get *A*'s in everything. 'Course, you do spend hours studying.

JAN: Yeah, that's about all I ever do. I like getting good grades, but there ought to be *something* else in life. I really thought high school was going to be a lot more fun than this!

CAROL: Me, too. Nothing but classes and homework. What a drag!

JAN (sighing): Life is pretty dull, all right. (Chanting.) We go to school, we go home, we do homework, we go to church, we go back to school, we go home, we go to church....Bor-r-ring!

BOTH (in unison, looking at each other): *Bor-r-ring!*

CAROL: Oh look, Jan! Look! Here comes the In-Crowd!

> *IN-CROWD enters from stage left, crosses diagonally behind the girls to opposite side of stage. They fold their arms and stand with body slanted toward one hip.*

JAN: Wow! They are *sooo* cool!

CAROL: And popular! Wouldn't you just die to be popular like that?

JAN: Are you kidding? Who wouldn't? Look! Where are they going now?

> *CROWD moves to back of stage and rolls up the legs of their jeans.*

CAROL: Maybe we ought to make ourselves more conspicuous so they'll know we're here.

JAN: Can't hurt to try.

> *Leaving their books on the bench, they edge a few feet towards center-stage. CROWD moves center-stage and puts neck-ties over T-shirts.*

CAROL: Ohhh! Far out! How'd they ever think of that?

JAN: Because they're *with* it, that's how. That's what it takes.

> *CROWD moves to position behind empty bench and puts on sunglasses. JAN and CAROL move to center-stage.*

JAN: I think they looked at us.

CAROL: Really? I can't believe it!

JAN: Really! Quick, put on your sunglasses and stand this way.

> *They put on sunglasses, stand with arms folded, leaning on one hip. They try to appear nonchalant. The crowd waves to them.*

JAN: Carol! They're waving at us! What do you think it means?

CAROL: They like us, that's what! Oh wow, they're coming over!

> *CROWD approaches, all exchange high-five hand slaps with the girls. CROWD moves to stage right, absorbing girls into the group. All put on headbands.*

JAN: Isn't this great? I've never had so much fun!

CAROL: Me neither. Wonder what they'll think of next?

JAN: I don't know, but whatever it is, it'll be a blast!

> *CROWD moves to stage left, roughing up their hair, dropping their suspenders to hang over their hips.*

CAROL: I wonder when they do their homework? All this running around takes up a lot of time. Not that it isn't fun, of course.

JAN: We probably won't have much time for homework from now on. Not if we want to keep up with these guys. You have to be dedicated.

CAROL: Yeah, I can see that. Hurry! We're going again!

> *GIRL walks across from stage right, reading a book. CROWD moves to center stage, crashing into her and knocking her down. CROWD doesn't stop moving, trampling over the girl to reach a new position, stage right. JAN and CAROL stop as the crowd leaves the fallen girl, running back to help her.*

JAN: Are you all right?

CAROL: Here's your book. I don't think it's hurt, just a little dirty.

GIRL: Oh, thank you. I'm okay, really. I just didn't see them coming. But I know that bunch. It doesn't pay to get in their way. They never look where they're going. Were you with them?

> *JAN and CAROL look ashamed, take off their sunglasses and headbands.*

JAN: I don't know if you'd say we were really with them....

CAROL: We were sorta hanging around them, but only for a little while.

GIRL: Hey, aren't you Jan Taylor? Sure, you're in my brother's history class. Don Riley. Know him?

JAN: Well, I know who he is. You're his sister? How'd you know me?

GIRL: He pointed you out once. He thinks you're pretty cool...says you're a brain! I think he likes you.

JAN: Wow! He said I'm cool? And he thinks I'm smart?

GIRL: Too smart to get mixed up in a crowd like that, that's for sure. Well, gotta go. Thanks for your help. See ya!

BOTH: Bye!

> *GIRL exits stage left as CROWD walks backward in a synchronized fashion offstage right. JAN and CAROL walk to the bench for their books.*

JAN: I guess the In-Crowd wasn't all we thought it would be.

CAROL: Yeah. They don't seem to care about much but themselves!

JAN: If that's what it takes to be popular, I'd rather not try.

CAROL: Well, you're still popular with me. And maybe with a guy named Don, too! (Teasing.) Did I get his name right? Hmm?

JAN: Real funny. Cut it out, Carol.

CAROL (laughing): Maybe he's got a brother.

JAN: Know what, Carol? You're pretty fun, even if you're not one of the In-Crowd. Hey, let's go to Bible study tomorrow night, okay? We haven't been all summer and—

CAROL: I know what you mean. I guess if we're going to follow anyone, it oughta be Jesus.

> *BLACKOUT (exit)*

Prayer Net
Barbara D. Larsen

Main Theme: Humility.
You may want to use this skit as a part of a study of Luke 18:9-14; James 4:6,10 or 1 Peter 5:6.

Characters
ANGEL CAPTAIN JOE SUNDAY
ANGEL SERGEANT BEN CHOSEN
A PHARISEE
A TAX COLLECTOR

Props: Two large police badges, a quill pen, a scroll, a beard, a long robe, a prayer shawl, a long tunic, a sash, a striped cloth, a headband. **Optional:** A low table, a cloth, a seven-branched candelabra, a loaf of bread, a pouch.

> *The scene is the Temple of Herod in Jerusalem. A low table covered with a rich cloth and set with a seven-branched candelabra and a loaf of bread is center stage. CAPTAIN JOE SUNDAY and SERGEANT BEN CHOSEN enter wearing white sheets with large police badges on their chests. BEN has a huge quill pen and scroll. They stand outside of the Temple.*

JOE (speaking in the clipped, no-nonsense manner of "Dragnet"): My name is Sunday. Joe Sunday. Angel Captain Joe Sunday, out of the Temple Precinct, Jerusalem. This is my partner, Angel Sergeant Ben Chosen.

> *BEN CHOSEN nods his head in greeting.*

We're working the Prayer Watch at the Temple of Herod. Lately there've been some disturbing reports about the quality of prayer going on here. Our job: observe and report.

BEN: That's our job.

JOE: That's what we're here for. What we want are facts. Just the facts, nothing else. Facts are what we're looking for. Prayer facts!

BEN: Right, Joe. If it isn't a fact, we don't want it.

JOE: You got it, Ben

BEN: I won't even write it down if it isn't a fact.

JOE: I wouldn't expect you to. That's what we're after, Ben. Facts.

BEN: You can say that again, Joe.

JOE: No I can't. That'd be saying it too much. We don't have time.

> *The PHARISEE, bearded and wearing a long robe and prayer shawl, struts on stage and enters Temple. The TAX COLLECTOR, wearing a long tunic with a sash, a striped cloth over his head tied with a headband and a pouch dangling from his waist, enters looking downcast. He stops before reaching the altar. JOE and BEN continue to talk while the PHARISEE kneels with exaggerated ceremony, adjusting robes and head covering, fiddling with prayer shawl, looking around before praying, recoiling in disgust when he sees the TAX COLLECTOR, who, with bowed head in hands, doesn't notice.*

JOE: Uh oh. I see two men going into the Temple now! They may be planning to pray in there. We'd better move in on them, Ben.

BEN: Affirmative.

JOE and BEN sneak into the Temple.

JOE: I think we've got them covered from here. What do you think?

BEN: Certainly seems like a good spot.

JOE: I like it. Not too close, not too far. Perfect, Ben.

BEN: Suits me fine. (He stares at the PHARISEE and grabs JOE's arm.) Say, I know that Pharisee! That's Solomon Levi! His family started that pants factory over in Jericho last year.

JOE: Yeah, I think you're right. That's him. That business isn't going anywhere from what I hear. Nobody in Judea wears those things. What'd you call them?

BEN: Pants.

JOE: That's it. Pants. Funny looking contraptions. Never catch on.

BEN: Never. Hey, Joe! Look! I think there's gonna be some praying.

JOE: About time. Be quiet, Ben, and listen.

PHARISEE (in a loud voice, using many gestures; raising arms to heaven): Jehovah God. Here I am again today, in your Holy Temple, just as I am every day. I'm not going about my many tasks, as other men are wont to do, forgetting You, not being faithful. Oh, I thank You that You didn't see fit to make me as other men. You have made me so much better! I'm really a credit to You, God. I never cheat people or steal anything. I never, never commit adultery, either! And You know Yourself how humble I am. What a joy for You to have a paragon such as myself come to pray to You! Remember, I've given you a tenth of all my earnings for years now. No paltry amount, either, You must agree! And twice every week I give up eating and fast. Just for You! I know You look down and see how holy I am

But that fellow over there, God, the one who came in when I did, the one who looks like a City Tax Collector....Lord God, I thank You that I'm not like him. (He shudders.) Oh no! Not a bit. You've really made me superior to him in every way, and don't think I'm not aware of it and so grateful!

And now, God, I must get on with my daily affairs. You can count on me to be back tomorrow, though, because this time I spend with You in prayer is such a blessing to us both. Amen.

PHARISEE stands, straightens garments and starts out. The TAX COLLECTOR creeps forward, falling to his knees in anguish before the altar, finally breaking down. The PHARISEE stops and listens.

TAX COLLECTOR: Oh, God! Have mercy on me, I beg of You! I'm not worthy to be in Your Holy Temple. I'm a sinner, Lord! A terrible sinner! Oh, forgive me. Will You forgive me? I'm so sorry! Cleanse me of my sin. Have mercy, Lord God, have mercy on me!

PHARISEE: Harrumph!

PHARISEE promenades out of the Temple. TAX COLLECTOR gets to his feet, dries off his tears and follows. They exit. JOE and BEN move to center stage, walking through the Temple doors.

JOE: There's a lesson there, Ben.

BEN: So? You learn something?

JOE: Yeah, facts, Ben. You got those facts down?

BEN (looking at notes): Got 'em all down, Joe.

JOE: Good. What'd you make of those prayers?

BEN: Well, can't say if Solomon Levi even got his prayer heard. But that last fellow, he really knew how to get right with God.

JOE: Exactly. One more thing, Ben.

BEN: What's that?

JOE: Basic heavenly truth, that's what. The man who makes himself great will be made humble....

BEN: And the humble man will be made great! I knew that, Joe.

JOE: Wish everybody did. Make our job a lot easier. C'mon, time to get back to headquarters and make our report. It's a long walk. Take us awhile.

> *They exit as BEN speaks.*

BEN: Why don't we fly this time, Joe?

> *BLACKOUT (exit)*

Evangelistic Skits

Evangelism and Skits: A Gentle Persuasion

It is common for people to resist persuasion. Something in us is wary of someone trying to convince us that what they have to say is true and important for our lives. Skepticism seems to be a by-product of the bombardment of advertising that the last few generations have been subjected to.

This resistance makes it difficult to relay even a message of hope. Not many want to open themselves to another advertisement. They put up their guard.

But there are ways to lower a person's guard. One example: people are more open to hearing new or challenging ideas if there is entertainment involved.

And if the medium of the skit is not entertainment, what is it?

Creative evangelism through skits has exciting possibilities. There are so many places to perform: malls, parks, street corners, amusement parks, bus stations, street fairs, convalescent homes, college campuses, hospitals, prisons and your own neighborhood are a few ideas.

Miming and clowning work great in many places. These forms of drama are attention-getting and fun. If you are promoting an upcoming event, dressing in costumes and handing out fliers to the public is an amusing way to advertise. And a lot of miming and clowning can be done without a script. Have your kids practice doing impromptu sketches until they get the hang of simply doing what comes to mind. One good exercise is to give them a Bible verse and see what they can come up with to perform for an unbelieving audience.

These evangelistic skits are for the express purpose of awakening an interest in Christ in the unbeliever. Once this interest is established, it can be followed up. You may want to give more concrete information and an invitation to come to a church event or make a decision for Christ. The skit players can transition from the skit to the information or invitation by making small talk with interested members of the audience.

One last thing: Although the skits in this section could be used in a youth meeting focused on outreach, they are primarily designed for street evangelism. These skits are not meant for church services. The target audience is the unbeliever, and unless your church caters to the unbeliever, the bulk of your church attenders are probably not non-Christians. Evangelism is bringing the truth about Jesus to those who do not know Him, so go and perform for them where they are.

Eternal Fire Protection

An Acts Drama Skit

Marco Palmer

Characters
EDDY: A tough street punk with a Brooklyn accent
MRS. GOLDSTEIN: A nasal New York housewife
FIREMAN CLINT: An unemotional, monotone, just-the-facts-ma'am guy
FIREMAN RAMBO: A macho, muscle-laden man of action

Props: About five red rocks, two fireman hats. **Optional:** A megaphone.

> *EDDIE runs on stage juggling four or five bright red rocks, blowing on his hands and shouting, "Ow woo hot hot hot WOH! YOUCH! HOT! HOT! HOT!" MRS. GOLDSTEIN, walking down the street, sees EDDY and lets out a bloodcurdling scream.*

MRS. GOLDSTEIN: Oh my goooosh! Oh my goooosh! This man's burning up! Somebody heeeelp! Somebody heeeelp!

> *Off in the distance the self-made siren sounds of FIREMEN CLINT and RAMBO are heard. The two run out, continuing to scream the siren noise, run around the audience, circle the stage, and come to a screeching halt in front of MRS. GOLDSTEIN.*

CLINT: What seems to be the problem here?

MRS. GOLDSTEIN (pointing frantically at EDDY): Are you blind? There's a man holding red hot rocks, and he's gonna burn up. You gotta help him! You gotta help him!

CLINT: Just the facts, ma'am. Just the facts.

MRS. GOLDSTEIN: I told you! (She shakes CLINT.) He's gonna burn up, and you gotta help him!

CLINT: We'll do our best, lady!

RAMBO (suddenly jumping out in front of the others): Stand back! We may have to hose him down!

> *MRS. GOLDSTEIN backs away and peers over the shoulders of the two firemen, watching the events with concern.*

CLINT (picking up a megaphone and shouting to EDDY): Don't be afraid, Mister! We're here to help you! Throw down those burning coals and we'll put them out and give you some first aid!

EDDY: No!

CLINT, RAMBO, GOLDSTEIN (together): No?! What do you mean, no?

EDDY: I said, No, ooh ooh hot hot.

CLINT: But you're burning up!

EDDY: Look everyone's a critic. Do I go around criticizing and bad-mouthing you, huh? Huh? Yo hot hot, ooh, oooh woh!

RAMBO (shouting to EDDY as if he were far away): But we're here...to help...you!

EDDY (sarcastically, mocking RAMBO): Why don't you mind...your own...business?!

CLINT: But those things could kill you!

EDDY: Hey, look. When I go, I go. I don't think about it.

RAMBO: Hey, do you mind if I have a look at those things?

EDDY: No, go right ahead.

>   *RAMBO takes off his hat, and EDDY dumps the rocks into it. While EDDY rests from his torment, the three gather around the open hat.*

RAMBO: Just as I thought!

CLINT and GOLDSTEIN: What?

RAMBO: *This*...is eternal fire! Even if we hosed it down, tossed it in the ocean, flew it to Alaska and threw it in the snow, this stuff never goes out! *It burns forever!*

EDDY: Shut up! (He snatches the rocks back and begins to juggle them.) Yo hot hot oooo yow woh!

CLINT: Mister, you're in big trouble! Get rid of this stuff now before it takes you with it!

EDDY: Cooooome on! It's not that serious! It's a just a way of life.

MRS. GOLDSTEIN: I don't know why you're holding on to those things, but what I wanna know is, how'd you get them in the first place?

EDDY: Well, I had this burning hatred for this person, and one of these showed up in my hands. Someone did me wrong, and I wouldn't forgive 'em and another one of these showed up! Then I had this burning jealously and I stole this hot rod and chased girls and did drugs and messed with occult stuff and all these things showed up in my hands.

CLINT: Don't you see? It's not going to stop! Even after you die, those things will keep burning you. God can't let you into heaven with those things!

EDDY: Hey...hey....Woh! I don't think a God of love would make me burn!

RAMBO: Is God making you burn now?

EDDY: Uh..., well, uh....No. I'm the one who's holding on.

RAMBO: God don't wanna make you burn!

CLINT: In fact, God sent His Son, Jesus to put out the eternal fire in people's hearts. He can put out your eternal fire, too, if you ask Him.

EDDY: Look! I'm a self-made man. This religion stuff burns me up! See ya. Ow ooo hot hot yow...

>   *EDDY exits still juggling the rocks.*

MRS. GOLDSTEIN: That's sad!

RAMBO: It sure is!

CLINT: Let's find someone who *wants* their fire put out!

>   *The FIREMEN start the siren and zoom off. MRS GOLDSTEIN runs after them.*

>   *EXIT (exit into audience to mingle)*

How to Fill an Empty Heart
Two Mime Skits
Judith L. Roth

Characters
EMPTY HEART: A non-Christian
FULL HEART: A Christian

Advance preparation: Prepare two black mime shirts so that one side of a red heart is sewn over the place on each shirt where a person's heart is. The red hearts should open like doors and fasten on the unsewn sides with velcro. The inside of each heart-door should be a pocket, able to hold a stuffed heart. (Ask someone who knows how to sew to help you if you don't know how to make this.) With fabric paint, print the word, "Jesus" on the space that will be covered by the heart-door. Make or buy two stuffed hearts that fit inside the heart pockets. See the illustrations below. FULL HEART will wear one of the mime shirts with the stuffed heart inside the heart pocket. EMPTY HEART will wear the other mime shirt with the heart pocket unstuffed.

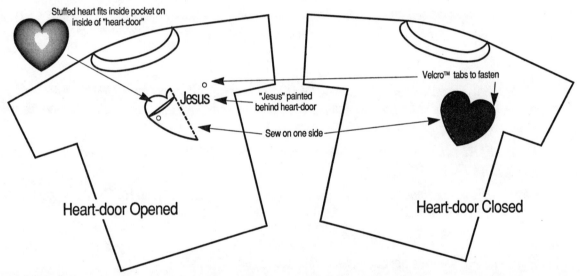

Stuffed heart fits inside pocket on inside of "heart-door"

Jesus

"Jesus" painted behind heart-door

Velcro™ tabs to fasten

Sew on one side

Heart-door Opened

Heart-door Closed

For convenience of writing, EMPTY HEART will be referred to as "him" and FULL HEART will be referred to as "her." Note: Because of possible jokes about the stuffed heart coming from a chesty person, it is probably best for FULL HEART not to be too chesty, and it may be better to have two males play the parts.

Mime Skit 1

EMPTY HEART goes up to FULL HEART and looks at her stuffed heart. He scratches his head, wondering why his heart is so empty in comparison to hers. He tries blowing into his heart to pump it up, but that doesn't work. EMPTY HEART thinks—perhaps he could fill his heart up with money. He pulls out an imaginary wallet, takes out the imaginary money and stuffs the money in his heart. His heart remains flat.

Perhaps EMPTY HEART could fill his heart with a car. He mimes admiring an invisible car, getting in the car, racing the car. He mimes making the car about the size of his heart and putting the tiny car in his heart. His heart remains flat.

Perhaps EMPTY HEART could fill his heart with human love. He mimes meeting a girl; a romantic interlude. He puts his finger in his heart and flutters it. But the heart remains flat.

Meanwhile, FULL HEART has been watching EMPTY HEART and shaking her head sadly. EMPTY HEART finally asks her (by pointing to the comparison between their two hearts and making questioning gestures) how he can have a full heart like hers. FULL HEART motions for him to follow her example.

FULL HEART prays; EMPTY HEART does likewise. She hugs him, slipping the extra stuffed heart into his heart-pocket (unnoticed by the audience, if this is possible). When EMPTY HEART notices that his heart is full, he becomes very happy. Carefully, he opens the outside heart to look inside. He is even more pleased to see Jesus inside.

EXIT (exit into audience to mingle)

Mime Skit 2

See the Advance Preparation for instructions on preparing for this skit.

FULL HEART is leaning against something. EMPTY HEART comes by, searching. He puts his hand up to shade his eyes, he gets out an imaginary magnifying glass, he peeks behind and beneath everything imaginable. EMPTY HEART finally looks beneath FULL HEART's feet, lifting them up one at a time.

FULL HEART pantomimes asking EMPTY HEART what he's looking for. EMPTY HEART mimes back that he's looking for love. (Some miming possibilities for love are: outlining a heart on his own chest, wrapping himself up in his arms, making an enraptured face.)

FULL HEART nods knowingly. EMPTY HEART asks FULL HEART if she knows where love can be found. FULL HEART nods.

EMPTY HEART becomes frantic, wondering where it is. He looks in FULL HEART's hair, behind her back, in her pockets, in her shoes, under her fingernails. No luck.

EMPTY HEART finally asks. Where?

FULL HEART opens up her pocket heart and shows Jesus inside.

EXIT (exit into audience to mingle)

Where's the Beef?

An Acts Drama Skit

Marco Palmer

Characters
OLD MCDONALD: A country hick farmer
HEFTY: Old McDonald's cow
LEROY: Old McDonald's hog
MCDEVIL: Satan
DUDE: An unbeliever
HILLBILLIES

Props: Hillbilly costumes, a cow costume, a rope, a pig costume, flashy male clothes, a devil costume.
Optional: A cigar, a liquor bottle.

A colorful jamboree of HILLBILLIES forms a semi-circle and begins an upbeat hand-clapping knee-slapping rap.

HILLBILLIES: Old McDonald had a farm. E I E I O. Uh.
And on this farm he had a cow. E I E I O. Uh.

HEFTY, an obese, bass-singing cow, enters shucking and jiving to the beat.

HILLBILLIES: It was a big cow!

HEFTY: The biggest baddest cow!

HILLBILLIES: It was a fat cow!

HEFTY: I'm the fattest now!

HILLBILLIES: And it loved to eat

HEFTY: Yes, I love to eat!
Give me a bail of hay, some grass to munch,
a trough of oats, and I'll have some lunch.

HILLBILLIES: And it ate from morning until the night.

HEFTY: With all my strength and all my might!

HILLBILLIES: That was its job—

HEFTY: To eat all day long.

HILLBILLIES: To get fatter and fatter—

HEFTY: I can do no wrong!

HILLBILLIES: But the cow didn't know what life was for.

HEFTY: And I don't care! Who could ask for more?

HILLBILLIES: All the cow's life it ate this hay
so in the end they'd haul him away.

The clapping abruptly stops. OLD MCDONALD enters wearing dirty farmer duds and carrying a rope. The HILLBILLIES sway back and forth sadly to an out-of-tune country-sounding melody that OLD MCDONALD "sings." HEFTY echoes with the same melody.

MCDONALD (in a piercing whine): Heeeeefty! You're comin' with me!
You weren't eatin' that hay for free!
Your time's run out! Your life is done!
There'll be parts of you on a hamburger bun!

HEFTY: Nobody warned me! I wasn't told
that my body was gonna be sold.
If I must go, I won't give you sass!
I just hope when I'm eaten, I give you gas!

OLD MCDONALD drags HEFTY off and the HILLBILLIES start rapping again.

HILLBILLIES: Old McDonald had a farm. E I E I O. Uh.
And on this farm he had a hog. E I E I O. Uh.

LEROY, an enormous gruff-sounding pig, enters wobbling to the beat.

This hog was nasty! This hog was gross!

LEROY: Heeey! I want some moldy toast!

HILLBILLIES: This hog was fat. This hog was smelly!

LEROY: I want somethin' bad to put in my belly!

HILLBILLIES: This hog ate anything under the sun.

LEROY: I want some garbage on a great big bun!

HILLBILLIES: This hog ate shoes, and even a shirt.

LEROY: I want mashed potatoes all covered with dirt!

HILLBILLIES: This hog ate things that hogs shouldn't eat.

LEROY: But I like eating fences. What a glorious treat!

As LEROY chews on an invisible fence post, the HILLBILLIES stop rapping. OLD MCDONALD enters. The chorus sways back and forth to whatever tune MCDONALD comes up with.

MCDONALD: Leroooy! You're making me tense!
Didn't I tell you not to eat my fence?
You've eaten the barn and my front door!
I can't afford to feed you no more!

LEROY: I wanted pig slop, but you were late!
I began to eat cuz I couldn't wait!

MCDONALD: Well, neither can I, you're not gettin' leaner.
It's time I made you into a wiener.

OLD MCDONALD drags LEROY away and the HILLBILLIES begin to rap.

HILLBILLIES: Old McDevil had a world. E I E I O. Uh. And on this world he had a man. E I E I O. Uh.

A pseudo-cool DUDE, decked out in his impressing-the-chicks threads bebops onstage, with cigar and whiskey bottle in hand.

He sinned all day long.

110

DUDE: Well, it's fun to do wrong!

HILLBILLIES: He cared nothing for God.

DUDE: God's somewhere, way up there,
      but I don't care—hell's no scare!

HILLBILLIES: So he did as he pleased.

DUDE: It's a life full of ease!

HILLBILLIES: And just like the cow got fat with the hay!

HEFTY (running out): He fattened himself for the judgment day.

> *HEFTY joins in on one side of the chorus line.*

HILLBILLIES: And just like the hog ate what was bad

LEROY (running out): He broke God's rules and made God mad.

> *LEROY also joins the chorus line at the opposite end from HEFTY. The clapping stops and MCDEVIL enters with a rope.*

MCDEVIL (rapping wickedly): Hey dude, you're coming with me!
      You didn't think you were sinning for free!
      You turned from God and served me instead.
      So I get your soul when you're dead!

DUDE: Hey man! This is all bunk.
      I never believed in that religious junk.
      I'll live my life just as I choose.
      I'll do what I want. How can I lose?

> *MCDEVIL laughs wickedly while dragging off the DUDE. The HILLBILLIES start the rap one last time.*

HILLBILLIES: So we hope you've listened to what we've said.
      Get it into your heart and into your head!
      See, if you choose the worldly way,
      you'll go "down there" come judgment day!
      You'll answer to God for the way you've lived,
      but if you ask, then He'll forgive!
      If you choose Christ to settle your score,
      you'll live with God forevermore!

> *EXIT (exit into audience to mingle)*

No One on Earth
A Melodrama
Judith L. Roth

Characters
SWEET CHARITY: The heroine
BUDLEY BELIEVER: The hero
NOGOOD NICK: The villian
MAMA: Charity's mother

Props: Unshelled peas, a pan, two sets of early 1900s clothes for women, a black cape, black clothes, a "hero" hat (fancy cowboy or Mountie hat).

> *MAMA is seated, shelling peas. CHARITY is pacing around the front room of the little farmhouse. Since this is a melodrama, all gestures and speaking lines should be exaggerated.*

CHARITY (distraught): Oh, Mama, Mama, what will I do? If I don't marry Nogood Nick we'll lose the farm and everything we've worked for.

MAMA: So marry him.

CHARITY: But if I marry him, I may be miserable for the rest of my life!

MAMA: So don't marry him.

CHARITY: But if I don't marry him, we'll have no place to go.

MAMA: So marry him.

CHARITY: But if I marry him, I'll probably wish I was dead!

MAMA: So don't marry him.

CHARITY: But if I don't marry him—

MAMA (cutting off CHARITY): Enough already! Sheesh! You're giving me a headache.

CHARITY (looking out window): Oh dear. There he is now. What will I do?

MAMA: Open the door.

> *CHARITY opens the door. NOGOOD NICK creeps vilely in dressed in a black cape and black clothes.*

NICK (in an oily voice; he pronounces his *r*'s as *w*'s): Dawling. How nice to see you. Awe you weady to be wed?

CHARITY: Weady to be what?

NICK: Weady to be wed. Awe you weady to be wed?

> *CHARITY looks questioningly at MAMA. MAMA shrugs her shoulders.*

CHARITY: Sure. I guess. Whatever.

NICK (ecstatically): Weally! How wondewful! We will mawwy today!

CHARITY: Mawwy?

112

NICK: You will be my bwide!

CHARITY: Your bwide?

NICK (putting his arms around CHARITY): Dawling. Tonight will be ouw fiwst night togethew.

CHARITY (finally understanding): Aaaaugh! Wait a minute. I didn't mean what you think I meant. Ooooh, get your gwubby hands off of me!

NICK: Gwubby?

CHARITY: I mean grubby. Get your grubby hands off of me and leave this instant!

NICK: So that's the way you want it, is it? You want to lose the fawm, be out on the stweets, die of stawvation?

CHARITY: Well, that's not exactly the way I want it.

NICK (sensing a reprieve): Think a minute, Sweet. (He puts one arm around her and makes a sweeping gesture with the other arm to indicate an imaginary scene. This is opposite to where BUDLEY will enter) Think. I could give you all youw little heawt desiwes. Money. Fame. Fowtune. And mowe.

CHARITY: Mowe?

NICK (moving to nibble on her neck): Lots mowe....

> BUDLEY enters looking wholesome and strong.

BUDLEY: Nogood Nick! I should have known.

NICK (snarling): You should have known what?

BUDLEY: That you would be here, preying on a sweet innocent girl.

NICK (chuckling evilly): She won't be innocent for long. She's going to mawwy me!

BUDLEY (to CHARITY): Is that what you want?

CHARITY: Are you kidding? But unless you have 3,000 dollars in your back pocket, he's the only way Mama and me have to survive.

BUDLEY: Garbage!

CHARITY: I suppose that's an idea. We *could* live off of garbage.

BUDLEY: That's not what I meant. I meant there are other ways to survive than marrying a nightmare.

NICK: Buzz off!

BUDLEY: Nope, the name's Budley. I'd say pleased to meet you, but I'm not. (Turning back to CHARITY.) There's Someone I want you to meet, little lady.

CHARITY: Who? Is it a loan shark? Maybe that would help.

BUDLEY: No, no, no. He's Someone who knows when you've been bad or good....

CHARITY: Santa Claus? You're going to introduce me to Santa? Hey, I could ask for a new place to live for Christmas.

BUDLEY: Ahem. No. Not Santa.

CHARITY (disappointed): Oh. Well, is it someone who could give me security like (makes face) Nogood Nick here?

BUDLEY: No one on earth can give you security—including Nogood. I want to introduce you to someone who's not from earth.

CHARITY: You know a space alien?

BUDLEY: Noooo.

NICK: Don't listen to him, Sweet. He's just twying to steal you away fwom me.

CHARITY: That doesn't sound like such a bad idea.

BUDLEY: You want fame and fortune?

CHARITY: That sounds good.

BUDLEY: Then marry Nogood. You want love?

CHARITY: Is this another trick question?

BUDLEY: If you want love and the security that comes from peace, come meet Someone.

NICK: Don't go! Think of the fawm. Think of the wealth. Think of ouw fiwst night togethew.

CHARITY (to BUDLEY): Quick! Where is this person?!

> *CHARITY rushes out the door in search of the Someone.*

MAMA: What are your intentions, young man?

BUDLEY (singing softly as he puts on his hat): Jesus loves me, this I know, for the Bible tells me so....

> *NOGOOD NICK cringes as he hears the words.*

MAMA: What's that got to do with the farm?

BUDLEY: There's more than one way to shell a pea, ma'am.

> *BUDLEY tips his hat to MAMA and exits, following CHARITY. MAMA drops her peas and follows BUDLEY.*

NICK: I'm doomed. (Desperately; to MAMA's retreating form) Hey lady, want to get mawwied?

> *EXIT (exit into audience to mingle)*

If I Die Before I Surf

Judith L. Roth

Characters
GARY: A Christian surfer
RICH: Gary's non-Christian surfing friend

Props: Two armchairs, a Bible, a flight bag.

> *GARY and RICH are seated side by side, facing the audience. They are in a plane headed for Hawaii. RICH is looking out the window. GARY is clutching the arms of the seat and appears to be quite nervous.*

RICH: Gnarly, dude. I think I can see the waves from here.

GARY (tensely): We're thousands of feet above the water, above the middle of the ocean. There aren't any waves, Rich.

RICH: Well, maybe it's Hawaiian cloud waves. Dude, that'd be a trip, cloud-surfing.

GARY (looking sick): Cloud-surfing.

RICH: Yeah. Like I'll bet that's how it's like when you jump off of cliffs with those big kite things....

GARY: You mean hang-gliding?

RICH: Yeah. Wow, maybe we should try that sometime.

GARY: I think that's something you're gonna have to do by yourself. Count me out.

> *RICH looks over and notices GARY's position.*

RICH: You're not nervous or anything, are you?

GARY: What makes you think that?

RICH: Man, you're strangling the seat.

> *GARY loosens his hold on the arms. He moves his head around, trying to loosen up his neck and shoulders.*

GARY: I'm all right.

RICH: Yeah, you're the one who's not afraid to die. Ha ha.

GARY: I'm not afraid to be dead, it's the pain involved in the process that bothers me.

> *They both suddenly jump and seem to be tossed about.*

What's that?

RICH: The seat belt light is on. Must be turbulence.

GARY: Just what I need.

RICH: Calm down, dude. It's just like...air pockets. Planes hardly ever go down because of air pockets.

GARY (sarcastically): Oh, that makes me feel *much* better.

RICH: Chill. Why don't you get out your Bible if you feel so terrible?

GARY starts rooting around under his seat. He pulls out his flight bag and digs through it.

What are you doing?

GARY: Looking for my Bible. (He finds it.) Got it.

RICH: I was kidding, man. Like that'll keep the plane in the air.

GARY: It'll get my mind on more important things.

RICH: Hey, if we're gonna die, I wanna know what's happening.

The plane hits another air pocket and GARY and RICH are tossed around violently. The turbulence subsides.

GARY: Yeah, so do I. Only I want to know what's happening with the part of me that's still gonna be around after the old body is gone.

More turbulence. This time they are really shaken up. Both have strangleholds on the arms of their chairs.

RICH: Hey, dude, maybe you better start praying.

GARY: Are you kidding? I haven't stopped praying since I stepped on the plane.

RICH: Fat lot of good that's done.

GARY: What do you know about it? I probably would have been a space case by now if—

RICH: Like I said, fat lot of good—

GARY: Hey, thanks for the encouragement, buddy.

RICH: Any time.

The turbulence seems to have stopped. GARY and RICH loosen their holds on the chairs and, together, shake out their bodies in relief.

GARY: You didn't really think we were going to die, did you?

RICH: What—die before we get to Hawaii? That'd be like the ultimate cruel joke.

GARY: No. The worst would be dying and not getting to heaven.

RICH: I thought Hawaii *was* heaven.

GARY tosses his Bible onto RICH's lap.

GARY: Looks like you've got some reading to do. (Pause.) Dude.

EXIT (exit into audience to mingle)

Mall Medley
Mall or Street Theater for Christmas
Lawrence G. and Andrea J. Enscoe

Characters
LITTLE KID #1
LITTLE KID #2
TEEN
BRIEL: An angel
CAROLERS: Teenagers

Props: A piece of paper and a pen, a stool, white clothing, a wide-beam flashlight. **Optional:** Sign that reads "XMAS EVE SALE!"

> *The CAROLERS are in a mall or on a streetcorner singing carols. They begin with "Joy to the World!" Next they sing, "O Little Town of Bethlehem," and finally, "O Come, All Ye Faithful." At the end of the last song, two of the CAROLERS move away from the group and assume the roles of LITTLE KID #1 and LITTLE KID #2. They raise their arms as if holding onto mother's hand. They look dazed, tired. They stand on one sore foot, then the other. CAROLERS hold up a sign that says, "XMAS EVE SALE!"*

LITTLE KID #1: Whaddid yer mom tell you before you guys went shopping?

LITTLE KID #2: She tole me, (mimicking) "Touch anything and you die." What about your mom?

LITTLE KID #1: She said, (mimicking) "One peep outta you and no presents on Christmas."

LITTLE KID #2: Wow. Did you peep?

LITTLE KID #1: No way! Not me! And I hadda peep all night.

LITTLE KID #2: Is this what Christmas is gonna be like all'a time? Gettin' pulled all over the place. Hearin' my mom use words I get spanked for.

LITTLE KID #1: Christmas was spozed to be fun. It *was* fun 'til we hadda start goin' shopping. Now I feel like I'm all in the way and stuff.

LITTLE KID #2: Yeah. Me too. I can't wait till it's all done.

LITTLE KID #1: Know what? Next year I'm gonna hide my mom's purse. I'm gonna bury it in the backyard. Then maybe we can do more singin' and stuff. Make some M&M cookies, me and her.

LITTLE KID #2: Yeah. And know what? I'm glad it's not *my* birfday. I sure don't want all everybody to be so mad and pushy on *my* birfday.

LITTLE KID #1: Yeah.

> *The CAROLERS begin singing "Away in the Manger." The LITTLE KIDS again assume their roles as CAROLERS and rejoin the group. The CAROLERS sing "What Child Is This?" next, and at the close of the carole, one CAROLER assumes the role of the TEEN and steps forward from among the CAROLERS. He begins poring over a list in his hand.*

TEEN: I'm waxed. Absolutely blown out. I got 20 people on my list and enough cash for about half of 'em. Man, Christmas was coming. I knew it, too. I should'a took that extra part-time job. I should'a made some major cash. So what if I flunk outta high school. College can wait. This is Christmas we're talking about! If I don't buy stuff I look like the cheapest geek in town. (He checks his list.) Well, I'm just gonna have to lose half'a these people. What else can I do? But how do I do it? I mean, my family—I can't blow them off. That's six right there. Okay, okay. Grandma. Hmmmm. I always get a card from her with five bucks in it. Been the same amount since I was eight. Who needs it? (He scratches off her name.) You're history, babe. Okay, okay. Mark and Tiffany? Are they gonna....Naw, they're not gonna get me anything. Total tight wads of the galaxy. (He scratches them off.) Later, dudes. Yeah, I better get Ashley something. That is if I *even* want her and me to see the light of prom night. Okay. (He looks over the list.) Uncle Yuke and Aunt Fanny. A wallet. Every year. With velcro. (He scratches them off.) Crash and burn. (He looks over the list.) Okay, from here down, history. (He tears the list almost in half.) Man, I get more nervous around Christmas than I do before my geometry exam. (To the audience.) Does that sound right to you? That the way it's supposed to be? Before I had any money, I use'ta make cards and stuff for people. Tell 'em I loved 'em and all. They all seemed happy with that. Man, I wish I was one'a those Wise Men. I'm tellin' you, they had it made, dude. (Pause.) They only had to buy for one.

The CAROLERS sing "We Three Kings of Orient Are" and "The First Noel." At the close of the carol, one of the CAROLERS assumes the role of BRIEL, comes out from among the CAROLERS and sits on a high stool. She is dressed in white pants and a white sweater and is holding a wide-beam flashlight that is not turned on.

BRIEL (looking down as if she is way up high): Look at 'em all down there! Running around, climbing the walls, looking for that one thing that'll make their lives bright. They don't know what bright is, let me tell you. They'll know soon enough, though. (She sighs.) I don't know. This whole manger idea. Do you think it's too light a touch? I mean, things are so hectic down there, I wonder if Bethlehem and a huddle of sleepy shepherds might get lost in the shuffle. Do you think? I don't know. You want to know what I like about it, though? It's completely different than anyone expected. It's very...human. The stable, smelly animals, a woman in labor. God is making a very...earthy entrance, if you ask me. And it makes for a pretty stark contrast, too. All that commotion going on down there and a group of half-asleep shepherds that never knew what hit 'em. (She looks down.) Half-asleep! What am I doing talking about it? It's time to move!

BRIEL stands up on the stool and looks down. She smiles and switches on the flashlight, shining it down like a spotlight.

Don't be afraid! I'm bringing you good news of great joy which will be for all people. Tonight in Bethlehem, a Savior has been born to you! (Luke 2:10-11)

BRIEL stays in position for a moment as the CAROLERS sing "Hark! the Herald Angels Sing!" She joins the other singers for "Angels We Have Heard on High." The CAROLERS finish the skit by singing "Silent Night."

EXIT (exit into audience to mingle)

The Old Box Routine

Lawrence G. and Andrea J. Enscoe

Characters
MIME
PANTO
FREEMIME

Props: Three mime outfits (black stretchy pants, black long-sleeved T-shirt), whiteface, a rag, red suspenders.

MIME, dressed in old-style black and whiteface, is performing the traditional "box" routine. He traces the flat of his hand along the dimensions of the large box he's trapped in—getting more and more disturbed as he finds no exit. He does this until a crowd gathers. PANTO, from an upper level of the mall or across the street, shouts at MIME.

PANTO: Come on! What're you doin' over there? Knock it off!

MIME stops and looks up. PANTO come down to where MIME is. PANTO is in a mime costume as well, but is wiping the clown white off his face with a rag.

Hey, you're not doin' that old mime stuff, are ya?! Come on. Get off it, will ya? That's older than Marcel Marceau. And even he don't do that stuff anymore.

MIME shows PANTO how he's trapped, flattening his hands against the invisible box.

Let me set ya straight, okay? First of all, most people don't like mimes anyway, all right? They're spooky. And second, people especially hate mimes that do the old "Stuck in the Box" routine. Old as the hills, you know what I mean?

MIME shakes his head frantically and continues showing PANTO that he's trapped.

You're not gonna say nothin', are ya? You're gonna play this to the hilt, aren't ya? (PANTO looks at the crowd.) What're ya gonna do? Mimes are not like normal people, y'know. All that zipped-lip treatment and putting on kabuki make-up in public does something to the brain. (To Mime.) You're not trapped in there. Look, I just stepped out of a box over there, okay? Ya don't need to do this. Trust me. Just step out.

MIME straightens and looks at him, incredulously.

Yes, it's true. Just walk out. One foot in front of the other. Like normal human beings. That's right.

MIME smiles and walks toward PANTO. He hits a "wall" of the box and falls back on his backside. MIME starts to cry.

Aw, don't do that! If there's one thing people hate to see a mime do, it's cry. Doin' the box is bad enough, but crying! Knock it off, I'm tellin' ya. That's better. (PANTO comes to the box.) I'm gonna show ya you're not trapped, okay? Watch this. (PANTO sticks his arm through the "wall." MIME looks wide-eyed.) See? Now here I go. I'm gonna step into your little invisible condo there and I'm gonna walk you out. Got it? Look out.

PANTO steps inside, then holds his hands up as if to say, "Voila!" MIME jumps to his feet, laughing and shaking his hand. PANTO yanks his arm.

Okay, let's go, Pasty Face.

PANTO trudges forward. He hits the "wall." MIME plows into him, falling on his backside again.

119

Not again! I don't believe it. Every time I think I'm out of a box, I get back into another one! *You!* (He turns on MIME, menacing him. MIME cringes.) You lured me in here because you didn't wanna be in here alone! That it?! Come on, help me find a way outta here. Don't just stand there! Start doin' the routine!

They flat hand around the dimensions. There appears to be no way out. Then FREEMIME enters, wearing the usual mime get up plus red suspenders. MIME sees him first. They mirror hands for a moment. Then MIME starts to call PANTO by waving, whistling and jumping up and down. MIME goes and tugs on PANTO's arm.

You found something? What is it, Lassie boy? You found a way—(He sees FREEMIME.) What is this?! Mime Central?! Get outta here. This is our space. Just move you and your box somewhere else, got it?

FREEMIME moves around freely, showing he's not confined.

Hey, what gives here? How come you're out of a box? You know somethin' we don't? Give us a hand, will ya? You see a way out from where you're standin'?

FREEMIME holds up a finger as if to say, "Watch me." He walks to one "wall," draws a large circle on the wall, grabs the circle and rolls it away.

That's impossible. Did you see that? Look at that big hole. He opened it up! Hey, you're not playin' mime games with me, are ya?

FREEMIME shakes his head. PANTO goes to the "hole" and sticks his hand through. He laughs. He sticks both hands through. He laughs some more. He steps his whole body through.

You did it! This is the life, isn't it. No more four walls! Say, who are you, anyway? (PANTO and FREEMIME stare at one another for a moment. Then FREEMIME holds out both palms. PANTO touches them in awe.) You don't say! It was *You* all the time! Of course...it all makes sense. (He turns to MIME.) Come on, Mr. Sunscreen, let's go. The Man with the Plan's here. The Creator! Don't you get it? The Box Breaker!

MIME is huddled up against one wall, shaking his head.

What's the matter? There's a hole there, can't ya see it? Don't tell me ya can't...ohhhh. You're one'a those, aren't ya? One'a the ones that likes looking for a way out but never wants to find it. That's too bad. (To FREEMIME.) You can't make 'im come out, can ya? (FREEMIME shakes his head.) I guess not. I'm ready. You lead the way, okay?

FREEMIME nods and goes off. PANTO walks to the "box."

(To MIME.) Don't stay in there too long, huh? The walls have a way of closin' in on ya. (In FREEMIME's direction.) Hey, wait up! (PANTO dashes off.)

MIME looks around nervously. He goes to the hole and peers out. He shakes his head and begins flatting his hand along the walls as in the beginning. After a moment, he just sits with arms folded.

Bow and EXIT (exit into audience to mingle)

Dr. Amos Grant
A One-Act Skit Based on the Early Music Sung by Amy Grant
Duffy Robbins

(If you would like the sheet music for the songs used in this skit, check your local Christian bookstore.)

Characters
NARRATOR
INTERN #1
INTERN #2
GENERAL HOSPITAL
NURSE #1
NURSE #2
FAITH
DR. AMOS GRANT
HUSBAND
PATIENT
DR. I. KEN SEE

Props: Hospital operating scrubs, a microphone, a white coat, a table for operating instruments, operating instruments (things such as scissors and tweezers), a hospital gurney, a clipboard, a pen.

> *INTERN #1 and INTERN #2 are outside the emergency room wearing scrubs and chatting quietly.*

NARRATOR (offstage, miked): Ladies and gentlemen, welcome once again to another nauseating episode of intrigue, romance and trash in..."General Hospital." As our scene opens this evening we see two young interns standing in the hallway outside the emergency room when they come face-to-face with the chief hospital administrator.

> *GENERAL HOSPITAL enters.*

INTERN #1: Attention!

> *Both interns snap to attention and salute.*

INTERN #2: Good evening, General Hospital.

> *GENERAL HOSPITAL, wearing a white coat, walks up to them quickly and salutes.*

How are you this evening, sir?

GENERAL HOSPITAL: Fine, thank you, Doctor—*generally* speaking. We've just gotten some important news, though. One of the top surgeons in the world is coming here to perform a special operation on a woman we just admitted for surgery. It is a very serious case; she has already been turned down by two other area hospitals—St. Elsewhere and Ain't Nowhere. Now it's up to us.

INTERN #1: Wow! That's big stuff. And you mean we're flying in the world renowned singing surgeon—the great, the awesome, the totally, totally renowned mega-skilled—

GENERAL HOSPITAL (interrupting): That's right. Dr. Amos Grant.

> *They exit together. NURSES #1 and #2 and FAITH enter and stand around an instrument table, organizing the operating instruments. INTERN #1 and INTERN #2 enter again and go towards the NURSES.*

NARRATOR: Later that same evening, the two interns join three nurses in the operating room as they await the arrival of the famous singing surgeon, the Bing of Bedpans, Dr. Amos Grant.

DR. AMOS GRANT enters.

AMOS GRANT: Good evening, nurses and doctors. I am Dr. Amos Grant, the world famous singing surgeon—I sing the notes while I cut their throats. Now please, where is the patient?

INTERN #1: She's on her way now, Doctor. Be patient.

AMOS: No, me not be patient. Me be doctor!

The PATIENT is rolled in. Her HUSBAND walks beside the bed, crying.

HUSBAND: Dr. Grant, I am so glad to see you. You've got to help my wife. She's got this strange illness that affects her eyes and her heart and her stomach. She keeps getting bigger and her heart is beating twice as much as a normal heart. Frankly, I'm wondering if she's going to make it....

Piano plays the introduction to "Will She Die?" This song is a parody of "El Shaddai." The words of "El Shaddai" were written by Michael Card; music by John Thompson. All NURSES and DOCTORS present sing the chorus through first. Then the HUSBAND talks through the chorus again while NURSES and DOCTORS hum solemnly in the background.

> Will she die? Will she die?
> Check her stomach and her eye.
> For days and days she's been in pain,
> you know, it's just a crying shame.
> Will she die? Will she die?
> I s'pose it's better her than I.
> Doctor bills are just so high.
> Will she die?

AMOS (immediately after song): Well, son, to tell you the truth, I don't know. You know how it is in the surgery game—you win some, you lose some and some get wheeled out. We'll never know if she'll live through this thing without giving it our best shot. Just a little joke there. Thought it might loosen you up to needle you a bit. Anyway, let's operate. I bet your wife's dying to find out what will happen. But first, let me introduce you to my colleague, an expert in optometry with degrees from several major schools—a man who was such a good student in eye surgery he was operated on once for a star pupil. In fact, he is so much into eyes that when he sent flowers to his girlfriend, he ordered irises. And he used to punish his children by giving them 40 lashes. Ladies and gentlemen, I present to you Dr. I. Ken See. Why don't you shake hands with our patient's husband, Dr. See.

DR. SEE enters and fumbles around shaking the air, then finally shakes the patient's foot.

HUSBAND: Here I am, Dr. See. I am the woman's husband.

DR. SEE: Oh, I see? (as in "icy")

HUSBAND: No, sir, not really. I'm quite warm. But my wife has been going back and forth with icy chills and hot fever. Tell me, will you able to save my wife's sight?

DR. SEE: I don't know, son. First, we'll have to check her eye sight. Tell me, have her eyes ever been checked?

HUSBAND: No sir, they've always been brown.

DR. SEE: Well, I'll have my nurse, Faith, check her out and test her sight. (Turns to nurse.) Faith, take her vision.

FAITH helps the PATIENT sit up and points offstage, silently asking the PATIENT eye-test questions, taking notes on a clipboard. The PATIENT needs help sitting and is obviously in pain.

HUSBAND: I sure hope you can fix her eyes, Doc. Ever since we've been dating, I've always liked her looks.

DR. SEE: Well, we'll soon see, son.

Piano plays the introduction to "What Bothers Eyes." This song is a parody of "Father's Eyes." "Father's Eyes" was written by Gary Chapman. DR. SEE begins singing the verse, then EVERYBODY joins DR. SEE on the chorus.

> I may not be the greatest doctor to do optometry,
> and my eye charts may not stir the hearts of all of those who see.
> But that's all right so long as when you leave you don't forget to pay,
> Cuz all my life with lights and charts I'll spend my every day...

Chorus:

> To see what bothers eyes,
> what bothers eyes....
> Eyes with stigmatisms, green or brown or blue,
> eyes that can't see near or far, and even crossed eyes, too.
> Eyes full of infection, or contacts causing pain.
> I use my charts to win their hearts
> so they can see again....

> **DR. SEE**: I see what bothers eyes,
> what bothers eyes,
> I see what bothers eyes.

HUSBAND: Boy, that was great. You ought to make a record. Do you have any contacts?

DR. SEE: No, as a matter of fact, I usually wear glasses. Just forgot to bring 'em today. But that's okay. I do better without them.

The PATIENT begins moaning loudly and FAITH helps her back to a lying position.

NURSE #1 (worried and urgent): Doctor Grant, the patient is sinking fast.

AMOS: Oh, good. I love music. What is she singing fast? Tell her to sing loud, too.

NURSE #2: Doctor, we better begin now. I think we're losing her. Oh no, her pulse has almost stopped entirely. She's going...going....

The DOCTORS and NURSES pick up instruments and make preparations to operate. PATIENT sits up quickly as piano plays pick-up notes to "The Pulse Is There." This is a parody of the song, "Don't Give Up on Me." "Don't Give Up on Me" was written by Brown Bannister, Amy Grant and Gary Chapman.

> Don't give up on me, I'm gonna make it
> I know it's hard for you to see
> Don't give up on me, cause I'm not fakin'
>
> If a part of me should keep me from dying
> start operating, you surely should be trying.
> The pulse is there so please don't give up on me.

> **EVERYBODY**: Don't give up on her, she's gonna make it.
> It sure is hard for us to see.

We can't give up on her, cause she can make it.
We can't give up on her, cause she can take it.
If a part of her should keep her from dying,
start operating and stop her husband crying.
The pulse is there—

PATIENT: Oh no, don't give up on me!

The PATIENT lies down and the DOCTORS and NURSES make operating motions.

NARRATOR: As our courageous team continues to operate, one of the nurses asks a simple routine question....

NURSE #1: Dr. Grant, have you ever operated on anyone before?

AMOS: Of course, Nurse. I just didn't get to look at the X rays before I began the operation. My wife wouldn't let me.

NURSE #2: Why not?

AMOS: Because they were x-ray-ed! Not really, I'm just ribbing you guys. Uh oh. Look, the patient is beginning to hemorrhage. Oh no!

Piano plays introduction to "Draining on the Inside." This song is a parody of "Raining on the Inside." "Raining on the Inside" was written by Kathy Troccoli and Amy Grant. AMOS sings slowly and thoughtfully.

When med scnool work was said and done
and I got my degree,
I thought that I'd make lots of dough
and spend it all on me.
And it's been fun to operate and work on people's hearts.
I get my kicks by doing tricks with people's vital parts.

EVERYBODY: But she's draining on the inside
Her heart wells up with blood that starts to pour
She's draining on the inside.
And if she dies of hemorrhaging—

AMOS: Then I'll be allowed to sing and cut no more

Well, I'll believe she'll make it.

DR. SEE: I agree with you, Doctor. You might say we see eye to eye! She'll make it, but only if she has a will to live. It's up to her, now. We've done all we can do. She'll have to will to live....

Piano gives note to begin immediately on chorus of "More Pain Reliever." This is a parody of the song, "I Have Decided." "I Have Decided" was written by Michael Card. EVERYBODY sings. PATIENT lifts her head to lead singing.

EVERYBODY: I have decided I'm gonna live despite my fever.
Just give me more pain reliever.
I'm gonna live 'cuz I believe.
I have decided that being dead makes me unable
to leave the operating table.
Don't wanna be stiff as a board.

PATIENT: For my health and things I must confess

I said I had no need,
but deep inside I felt a pain
and soon I began to bleed.
'Cuz a germ inside kept killing me
but I didn't want to die.
And now the doctor's made it clear to me
I won't have to say bye-bye.

EVERYONE: (repeat chorus)

NURSE #1: Well, Doctor, that's just about it. Should we sew her up?

AMOS: Suture self. Get it? Sorry. Guess I'm just an old sew and sew. No wonder everybody calls me a Singer.

NURSE #2: Boy, Doctor, you're sure funny. You're keeping us in stitches.

AMOS: Thanks, Nurse. You're not bad yourself. Tell me, how long have you been in nursing? Didn't I see you working in here cleaning counters as a maid last week?

NURSE #2: Yes, Doctor. That was me. You see, I really prefer being a cleaning woman, but the hospital said they needed me to be a nurse.

Piano plays introduction to "Counter Top." This song is a parody of "Mountain Top." "Mountain Top" was written by Brown Bannister.

NURSE #2: I like to clean and I like to spray,
I'll take sponges and dust cloths any old day.
I go to the broom closet and I want to stay—
a syringe and blood test just isn't my way.

EVERYBODY: Oh, I'd love to clean off the counter top,
I'm happy sweeping up the floor.
I'd love to clean off the counter top
'Cuz with shots I make the people sore.
But I have to quit wiping the counter top
and quit thinking 'bout the floor below.
It's true I don't know how to cut or sew
but it's nurses that they need more

(Repeat last two lines.)

HUSBAND (looking at PATIENT): Look, Doctor, what's that? Her stomach is moving.

DR. AMOS pulls out a baby doll that was hidden behind the patient.

What did you take out of her? What is that crying? Hey, what's going on?

AMOS: Well, son, it turned out not to be cancer after all. Congratulations!

Piano plays the introduction to "She's Only Pregnant." This song is a parody of "Fat Baby." "Fat Baby" was written by Steve Millikan and Rod Robison.

AMOS: Calm yourself, man. Take a minute or two.
You won't believe this, but I tell you it's true.
You brought your wife in here, thinking this was the end.
She's saved, but that's just where surprises begin.
You worried her tummy was growing too much,
and toward the end she had to walk with a crutch

But today all us doctors did our very best
And what a surprise to find that you have been blessed—

EVERYBODY: With just a fat little baby.
She's only pregnant and we don't mean maybe.
I'm glad you knew to seek a doc's advice
because dying leaves you cold as ice.

She's been x-rayed, diagnosed, tested for blood.
And if we had blown it, our names would be mud.
And now it looks like a baby, at three pounds sixteen.
He's the ugliest kid that we've ever seen.

We know that's a horrible thing to say.
We hope you're not so mad that you decide not to pay.
Just remember, while she's laying in bed,
that motherhood sure beats being dead.

(Repeat Chorus.)

HUSBAND: Wow, Doctor, how can my wife and I ever thank you? I can't believe it—she's alive!

Piano plays introduction to "What a Difference You've Made in My Wife." This song is a parody of What a Difference You've Made in My Life." "What a Difference You've Made in My Life" was written by Archie P. Jordan.

What a difference you've made in my wife
just by using your surgical knife.
You're the greatest doctor alive.
Oh what a difference you've made in my wife.

EVERYBODY: What a change you've made in her heart.
What a change you've made in her heart.
You replaced all the broken parts.
Oh what a difference you've made—
(Music repeats above line twice)

AMOS: With just my surgical knife.

EVERYBODY: Oh what a difference we've made in his wife.

BLACKOUT (freeze, then exit)

Topical Index